UNDERSTANDING
SAM SHEPARD

UNDERSTANDING CONTEMPORARY AMERICAN LITERATURE
Matthew J. Bruccoli, Founding Editor
Linda Wagner-Martin, Series Editor

Volumes on

Edward Albee I Sherman Alexie I Nelson Algren I Paul Auster
Nicholson Baker I John Barth I Donald Barthelme I The Beats
Thomas Berger I The Black Mountain Poets I Robert Bly
T. C. Boyle I Raymond Carver I Fred Chappell I Chicano Literature
Contemporary American Drama I Contemporary American Horror Fiction
Contemporary American Literary Theory
Contemporary American Science Fiction, 1926–1970
Contemporary American Science Fiction, 1970–2000
Contemporary Chicana Literature I Robert Coover I Philip K. Dick
James Dickey I E. L. Doctorow I Rita Dove I John Gardner I George Garrett
Tim Gautreaux I John Hawkes I Joseph Heller I Lillian Hellman I Beth Henley
James Leo Herlihy I John Irving I Randall Jarrell I Charles Johnson
Diane Johnson I Adrienne Kennedy I William Kennedy I Jack Kerouac
Jamaica Kincaid I Etheridge Knight I Tony Kushner I Ursula K. Le Guin
Denise Levertov I Bernard Malamud I David Mamet I Bobbie Ann Mason
Colum McCann I Cormac McCarthy I Jill McCorkle I Carson McCullers
W. S. Merwin I Arthur Miller I Lorrie Moore I Toni Morrison's Fiction
Vladimir Nabokov I Gloria Naylor I Joyce Carol Oates I Tim O'Brien
Flannery O'Connor I Cynthia Ozick I Suzan-Lori Parks I Walker Percy
Katherine Anne Porter I Richard Powers I Reynolds Price I Annie Proulx
Thomas Pynchon I Theodore Roethke I Philip Roth I May Sarton
Hubert Selby, Jr. I Mary Lee Settle I Sam Shepard I Neil Simon
Isaac Bashevis Singer I Jane Smiley I Gary Snyder I William Stafford
Robert Stone I Anne Tyler I Gerald Vizenor I Kurt Vonnegut
David Foster Wallace I Robert Penn Warren I James Welch
Eudora Welty I Tennessee Williams I August Wilson I Charles Wright

UNDERSTANDING

SAM SHEPARD

James A. Crank

The University of South Carolina Press

Published by the University of South Carolina Press
Columbia, South Carolina 29208

www.sc.edu/uscpress

Manufactured in the United States of America

21 20 19 18 17 16 15 14 13 12   10 9 8 7 6 5 4 3 2 1

Library of Congress Cataloging-in-Publication Data

Crank, James A.
   Understanding Sam Shepard / James A. Crank.
      p. cm. — (Understanding contemporary American literature)
   Includes bibliographical references and index.
   ISBN 978-1-61117-106-8 (cloth)
   1. Shepard, Sam, 1943– —Criticism and interpretation. I. Title.
PS3569.H394Z668 2012
812'.54—dc23

                                        2012021977

This book was printed on a recycled paper with 30 percent
postconsumer waste content.

For Jeff, my anchor

CONTENTS

SERIES EDITOR'S PREFACE

The Understanding Contemporary American Literature series was founded by the estimable Matthew J. Bruccoli (1931–2008), who envisioned these volumes as guides or companions for students as well as good nonacademic readers, a legacy which will continue as new volumes are developed to fill in gaps among the nearly one hundred series volumes published to date and to embrace a host of new writers only now making their marks on our literature.

As Professor Bruccoli explained in his preface to the volumes he edited, because much influential contemporary literature makes special demands, "the word *understanding* in the titles was chosen deliberately. Many willing readers lack an adequate understanding of how contemporary literature works; that is, of what the author is attempting to express and the means by which it is conveyed." Aimed at fostering this understanding of good literature and good writers, the criticism and analysis in the series provide instruction in how to read certain contemporary writers—explicating their material, language, structures, themes, and perspectives—and facilitate a more profitable experience of the works under discussion.

In the twenty-first century Professor Bruccoli's prescience gives us an avenue to publish expert critiques of significant contemporary American writing. The series continues to map the literary landscape, and provide both instruction and enjoyment. Future volumes will seek to introduce new voices alongside canonized favorites, to chronicle the changing literature of our times, and to remain, as Professor Bruccoli conceived, contemporary in the best sense of the word.

Linda Wagner-Martin, Series Editor

ACKNOWLEDGMENTS

I am most thankful to Linda Wagner-Martin, whose guidance of this manuscript from first inception through final product is indicative of the generosity and kind spirit I grew to admire so much during my time in Chapel Hill. Her advice and mentorship have meant more to me than I can possibly articulate. I am lucky to have been her student and even luckier to now be her friend.

Thanks, too, must go to my family, friends, and colleagues at Northwestern State University for their consistent support throughout the run of this manuscript. Special thanks go to Jackie M. Hawkins and the staff at Watson Library and to those who helped with this manuscript, from copyediting to reformatting to offering suggestions: Phyllis Agnew, Jeff Ware, Linda Angell, Bruce E. Ford, Barry Schwarz, Julie Kane, Mack Fritch, and others, you have my heartfelt gratitude. Your work is much appreciated.

My sincere appreciation also must go to my editor, Jim Denton. His help in key places throughout this volume was invaluable.

UNDERSTANDING
SAM SHEPARD

CHAPTER 1

Understanding Sam Shepard

"It seems that the more you write, the harder it gets, because you're not so easily fooled by yourself anymore," wrote Sam Shepard. "Even so, writing becomes more and more interesting as you go along, and it starts to open up some of its secrets. One thing I'm sure of, though. That I'll never get to the bottom of it."[1] In writing about his process of composition, dramatist Sam Shepard expressed the central ideas of his plays: exposing secrets, opening up hidden spaces to understand one's identity, and searching endlessly for satisfying conclusions. His plays investigate complicated worlds that seem to deepen with each new performance. For the uninitiated, his work may appear dense and rough: characters in his plays may speak, act, or move spontaneously and illogically. Shepard's language, including his copious stage directions, can seem stylized and needlessly complex; his dialogue is alternately lyrical and elaborate without context or exposition; and his realistic characters frequently interact unexpectedly and inexplicably with imaginary figures. Consequently he may frustrate readers more used to linear plots and realistic characters. Sam Shepard is, in short, a difficult playwright to understand.

But scholars, students, directors, actors, and dramaturges who approach the man and his work thoughtfully discover an incredibly rewarding and focused vision, one that has enthralled audiences and critics alike since his plays first exploded onto stages in New York during the 1960s. During his nearly fifty-year career, Sam Shepard's work has consistently documented the ever-changing cultural landscape of America: from its obsessions with rock 'n' roll and a mythic West to the realities of its class consciousness and broken families. He frequently challenges Americans' self-perceptions by exposing lies and secrets inherent in them, and his plays reexamine solved mysteries of the theatrical world—language, form, myth, narration, spectator, character—and defy audiences' expectations by violating their conventions.

Now, nearly a half century after the premiere of his first play, Sam Shepard still remains at the forefront of the American theatrical scene as one of our most prolific, thoughtful, and challenging living playwrights. Shepard has written nearly fifty plays while thriving as an actor, director, and producer for the stage, television, and cinema. Theater critics have proclaimed him "the most ruthlessly experimental and uncompromising" American playwright and "the greatest American playwright of his generation." His plays articulate America's anxieties and fears during very specific historical and cultural moments. Yet, like the works of the great American playwrights before him, Shepard's plays find new audiences in successive generations. They are admired by scholars and actors alike. Literary critics admire the structure of his works, and some of the finest stage and screen actors, including John Malkovich, Gary Sinise, and Kathy Bates, have been eager to play parts in them because the emotional evolution of his characters provides opportunities for experimentation.

Although watching a Sam Shepard play is engaging, reading his plays for the first time may prove daunting. Because Shepard is clearly influenced by the theater of the absurd dramatists (such as Pirandello, Beckett, and Ionesco), his work can seem dense and incomprehensible to first-time readers without an understanding of absurdist techniques. This study introduces scholars, students, and directors to the challenging issues taken up in Shepard's plays, including experiments with language, setting, and characters. One key to understanding the works of Sam Shepard is his life. To a greater degree than those of most other American dramatists of his generation, his plays are largely autobiographical. Consequently information about his life facilitates understanding of his art. Because many of his plays focus on the American family, understanding Shepard's early family life becomes even more important in unlocking the mystery of his craft.

Samuel Shepard Rogers III was born in Fort Sheridan, Illinois, in 1943 to U.S. Army Air Force pilot Samuel Shepard Rogers II and Jane Elaine Shepard. Shepard remembers the town as "a real fort, where army mothers had their babies" while the men were stationed abroad. Their time in Illinois was short, however, because the family moved often throughout the United States—to South Dakota, Utah, and Florida. Eventually the family settled on an American base in Guam. Shepard's memories of his time there revolve around his discovery that language has political import and can have the potentiality for violence: "There were a lot of Japanese on the island, who had been forced back into living in the caves, and they would come down and steal clothes off the clothes-lines, and food and stuff. All the women were issued army Lugers, and I remember my mother shooting at them. At that time everyone referred to Oriental people or Philippino [*sic*] people as gooks, and it wasn't until the Vietnam War that I realized that gook was a derogatory term—it had just been part of the army jargon, all the kids called them gooks, too."[2] The turbulence of his life abroad with his father gave way to a more normal calm when his family settled in Pasadena, a suburb that in some ways resembled a small town but stood in the shadow of Los Angeles, the largest city in the American West.

There Shepard would come to find one of his great muses: the interior world of the white, middle-class American family. Shepard remarked that Pasadena was "not all that rich, but very proud of the municipal swimming plunge and the ice-skating rink, and all that small-town-America-type stuff." The young Sam Shepard (known as "Steve" to family and friends) lived in Pasadena from ages five to eleven. At home his father bordered on being a despot. Shepard recalls his being "very strict, . . . very aware of the need for discipline, so-called," and the boy felt his creativity threatened often by his father. "It was really like being jailed," he once said of his father's demanding rules.[3] As he moved into his teenage years, he and his father constantly butted heads in power struggles in front of the whole family. Sam's sister, remembering their relationship, said they were "like two pit bulls" vying to see who was the alpha dog: "You put two virile men in a room and they're going to test each other."[4] Ruthless struggles for power within the family would later appear in Shepard's plays where characters fight for some measure of autonomy within suffocating family structures.

Eventually Shepard's family moved from the picturesque, sleepy town to a much more rugged life on an avocado ranch in Duarte, California, fifteen miles from their old address. The move suited Sam, who felt more at ease in the country and away from the stuffy suburban atmosphere of Pasadena: "I really liked being in contact with animals and the whole agricultural thing. . . . It was a funny community, divided into three very distinct social groups. There were the very wealthy people, who had ranches up in the mountains with white-faced Hereford cattle roaming around, and swimming-pools and Cadillacs. And then you'd get these very straight middle-class communities, people who sold encyclopedias and stuff like that." Shepard was amazed at the division between the middle class and the working poor, who were mostly black or Mexican and who, like the "gooks" of Guam, were segregated from the rest of the community: "It was the first place where I understood what it meant to be born on the wrong side of the tracks, because the railroad tracks cut right down through the middle of this place: and below the tracks were the blacks and Mexicans."[5]

Sam was a good student at school, though he admitted to experimenting with Benzedrine and hanging out with the wrong crowd. Despite his bravado he had a deep love for animals and considered becoming a veterinarian. Outside school he was a member of the 4-H club, and a ram he raised placed first in the Los Angeles County Fair. Although his adolescence was far from ideal, he would come to reminisce fondly about his "pastoral" years in Duarte and would use the settings and characters from his boyhood and adolescence in plays such as *Curse of the Starving Class, The Tooth of Crime,* and *The Unseen Hand.* He would also plumb the depths of his power struggles with his father to create some of the most compelling moments in his oeuvre.

During his time at the small junior college Mount San Antonio in Walnut, California, he first began experimenting with the theater. He acted in the school's productions of *Harvey* and *The Skin of Our Teeth* and even wrote his first play, "a sort of Tennessee Williams imitation, about some girl who got raped in a barn and her father getting mad at her or something."[6] Shortly after his first experiment writing a play, Shepard got involved as an actor in the Bishop's Company Repertory Players, with whom he toured the East Coast putting on one-night productions of plays in churches. In the traveling company, Shepard learned a valuable lesson that he would come back to throughout his career: "Anybody can make theater. You don't need to be affiliated with anybody. You just make it with a bunch of people."[7] Shepard followed his new passion for theater all the way to New York City, where he tried unsuccessfully to become a professional actor. There he found himself involved with a "really exciting music scene. The world I was living in was the most interesting thing to me, and I thought the best thing I could do maybe would be to write about it, so I started writing plays."[8]

In 1964, while working at the nightclub Village Gate, Shepard wrote the first of his plays ever to be produced. The play owed a debt to experimental theater, to the theater of the absurd, and to an early exposure to the works of Samuel Beckett, which had changed his writing style. When he first encountered the playwright's *Waiting for Godot,* he said it was "like nothing I'd ever read before. . . . And I thought, what's this guy talking about, what is this?"[9] From the influence of Beckett's aesthetic, Shepard wrote the short, semi-absurdist one-act *Cowboys,* so titled because he and his close friend Charles "used to run around the streets playing cowboys in New York. We'd both had the experience of growing up in California, in that special kind of environment, and between the two of us there was a kind of camaraderie, in the midst of all these people who were going to work and riding the buses." *Cowboys* became a powerful meditation on youth, innocence, and the incessant need for adventure—things to which the young Sam Shepard, as a new immigrant from California, could easily relate. Because of his roots in the West, he was also acutely aware of the cowboy's mythic hold on the American popular imagination: "Cowboys are really interesting to me—these guys, most of them really young, about 16 or 17, who decided they didn't want to have anything to do with the East Coast, with that way of life, and took on this immense country, and didn't have any real rules."[10] As a stranger in a far away land without rules, Shepard felt a deep connection with the image of the cowboy.

The idea that anyone would perform his plays initially frightened Shepard, but when the headwaiter at the Village Gate nightclub told him that he was looking for fresh material for a new venture he called Theatre Genesis, Sam showed him the draft of his play about cowboys. During rehearsals for *Cowboys,* Shepard decided to add another short one-act play, *The Rock Garden,* to the evening's bill. Despite some early, negative reviews, critic Michael Smith of the *Village Voice* validated Shepard's decision to move to New York; Smith wrote that Shepard explored new territory for the American dramatist, "an area between ritual and naturalism, where character transcends psychology, fantasy breaks down literalism, and the patterns of ordinariness have their own lives. His is a gestalt theater which evokes the existence behind behavior."[11] The high praise from one of the most influential critics in New York won Shepard instant credibility and fame.

Following the modest success of his two one-acts, Sam Shepard began writing plays at a feverish pace and often wrote countless plays in a week's time. "I used to write very fast," he admitted to an interviewer. "The stuff would just come out, and I wasn't really trying to shape it or make it into any big thing. . . . I would have like a picture, and just start from there. A picture of a guy in a bathtub, or of two guys on stage with a sign blinking—you know, things like that."[12] Shepard's prolific period happened to coincide with the emergence of the "off-off-Broadway" movement of the early 1960s in the wake of which small, avant-garde plays were capturing the imagination of audiences. The more intimate productions provided an alternative to the huge, expansive Broadway pieces running at the time. Shepard remembers the movement as full of possibilities: "On the Lower East Side there *was* a special sort of culture developing. . . . I mean nobody knew what was happening, but there was a sense that something was going on."[13] Because he wrote so many compelling plays in such a short period, some of which were running simultaneously, he quickly found a place beside LeRoi Jones, Edward Albee, and Lanford Wilson, the major American playwrights at that time.

Shepard's plays in the mid-1960s drew enthusiastic crowds and impressed critics. *Up to Thursday, Dog, Rocking Chair, Three and Melons, 4-H Club, Chicago, Icarus's Mother,* and *Red Cross* all opened during the first part of the decade. The latter three earned him his first Obie awards. The one-acts shared the same stripped-down aesthetic and nonnaturalistic expression that would come to be recognized as hallmarks of his early work. One critic noted the difference between a conventional play, where "the characters stay pretty much the same over the time span of the play, which could be two days or twenty years," and Shepard's early, experimental plays, where characters frequently shift personalities from one monologue to the next. And the language they speak is specific, too. Each character engages in "purposefully banal dialogue to stitch together images, actions, and comically/poetically extended monologues which puncture the surface of the theatrical event."[14] Each early one-act contains a heightened expressionistic style that draws upon his experiences, from his childhood and adolescence to his more recent move across the country to live in abject poverty surrounded by bohemians and artists. Shepard later explained why his early writing draws so much from his past: the plays "come from all kinds of things, they come from the country, they come from that particular sort of temporary society that you find in Southern California, where nothing is permanent, where everything could be knocked down and it wouldn't be missed, and the feeling of impermanence that comes from that—that you don't belong to any particular culture[,] . . . the more distant you are from [where you grew up], the more the implications of what you grew up with start to emerge."[15] Shepard's short, early one-acts were also heavily influenced by his new friendship with Joe Chaikin, the founding father of the experimental Open Theater, whose repertory cast included Shepard's then girlfriend Joyce Aaron. Chaikin's group sought to explore "techniques for performing nonnaturalistic material, the Brechtian plays and verse dramas that irresistibly attract the avant-garde."[16] Chaikin and Shepard's friendship flourished because of their shared interest in the avant-garde.

Shepard later admitted that he found it difficult "to remain with a certain attachment" to his early, experimental plays: "I write plays before I get to another kind of play, and each play may be a sort of evolution to something else. I always feel like leaving behind rather than hanging on to them."[17] Shepard's evolution manifested itself in the form of his first full-length piece, entitled *La Turista* (1966), which was performed at the famous American Place Theater. The play explored cultural myths about America and Mexico and contained a subtle satire on the persistence of stereotypes about indigenous people. After it was performed, Shepard's interest shifted from the obsessions he indulged in the early one-acts to a visceral aesthetic highly influenced by American rock 'n' roll music. Biographer Don Shewey has argued that Sam Shepard's next eight plays—*Shaved Splits, The Unseen Hand, Operation Sidewinder, The Holy Ghostly, Black Dog Beast Bait, Mad Dog Blues, Cowboy Mouth,* and *The Tooth of Crime*—all "recall the poetically evocative but inscrutable names of famous rock bands and albums from the sixties."[18] In addition to his duties as a playwright, Shepard performed in several 1960s rock 'n' roll bands, including the locally famous Holy Modal Rounders, for whom he was the drummer. He joined the band in the recording studio and on their West Coast tour.

In 1970 Shepard married O-Lan Johnson, whom he had met through Theatre Genesis. A few months later their son Jesse Shepard was born. The relationship between Shepard and O-Lan was rocky from the beginning. Shortly after their marriage, Shepard began a brief, torrid affair with rock star Patti Smith. Their affair would become mythologized in the play *Cowboy Mouth*, a collaborative piece written by Shepard and Smith. *Cowboy Mouth* combines elements of documentary and mythology into a highly subjective look at the strange relationship between Smith and Shepard: in it both authors explore emotional responses to their blossoming affair and its inevitable disintegration. Though Shepard originally cast himself as the central protagonist in the play, the role became too personal for him to sustain. He quit after the previews of the play; he would later admit that "the thing was too emotionally packed. . . . I suddenly realized I didn't want to exhibit myself like that, playing my life onstage. It was like being in an aquarium."[19]

Cowboy Mouth was important in establishing two central elements of Shepard's bourgeoning aesthetic: weaving together autobiography and fiction and exploring the intersection of character and sound. Shepard believed that he could use music to bring the audience to a greater understanding of character. He later argued, "I think music's really important, especially in plays and theatre—it adds a whole different kind of perspective, it immediately brings the audience to terms with an emotional reality. Because nothing communicates emotions better than music, not even the greatest play in the world."[20] Shepard worked briefly for the Italian director Michelangelo

Antonioni as script doctor for the film *Zabriskie Point,* and his next major play, *Operation Sidewinder,* in which he included ten original songs, bears the mark of his complicated work with Antonioni. *Sidewinder*'s convoluted plot involves black nationalists, dim-witted tourists, and a self-aware computer disguised as a snake. The final production was a disaster. The premiere of the play at Lincoln Center frustrated Shepard, who argued that the director had badly misunderstood what he was trying to do with the music and had, instead, turned the play into a grotesque spectacle.

Even with the bad taste in his mouth from *Operation Sidewinder,* Shepard continued to work to integrate text, sound, and music (especially rock 'n' roll music) into drama. His next series of plays (culminating in *The Unseen Hand*) explored ways in which music might not only connect audiences with characters but also create mythologies of its own. Each of these later "musical texts" was also grounded in Shepard's own life experiences.

While the incendiary buzz of his affair with Patti Smith (and its lurid recapitulation in *Cowboy Mouth*) began to spread, Shepard left Smith, New York, and the off-off-Broadway movement that he had helped to spark and went to live for three years in England. There he attempted to relearn the mythology of the American identity: "When I first got to New York it was wide open, you were like a kid in a fun park, but then as it developed, as more elements came into it, things got more insane—you know, the difference between living in New York and working in New York became wider and wider. . . . I didn't feel like going back to California, so I thought I'd come [to England]—really get into music, you know. . . . I had this fantasy that I'd come [to England] and somehow fall into a rock 'n' roll band. It didn't work."[21] Although Shepard's dream of becoming a rock 'n' roll star fell through, he found that his ability to piece together the mystery of being an American was easier away from the United States. Within a few months he had finished the first draft of what would become one of his most famous plays, *The Tooth of Crime.*

The setting, like that of Beckett's *Waiting for Godot,* is sparse and vacant save for a small chair in the middle of the stage. The play's second act is a rock 'n' roll duel between the main character, Hoss, an almost-famous rock star who is beginning to second-guess the music business and its accompanying annoyances, and Crow, a Keith Richards look-alike who can imitate Hoss's style down to his signature moves. The play's dizzying stream-of-consciousness dialogue includes frequent references to American pop music and employs the idioms of British youth culture slang in the early 1970s. Critics found in *The Tooth of Crime* Shepard's response "to Altamont, to Charles Manson, to the relentless litany of assassinated leaders, overdosed rock stars, picked-off Black Panthers, and all the other end-of-the-sixties death scenes that run together into one bloody blur."[22] Most important, it is the first of Shepard's plays to have a linear plot and follow the conventions of dramatic trajectory by including a climactic duel between Crow and Hoss.

Whereas in *Operation Sidewinder* and *The Unseen Hand,* Shepard had used music to elucidate the words that were being spoken onstage, in *The Tooth of Crime* he used it to distract the audience from them. In this play Shepard explored the idea of music as disrupter: "I wanted the music in *Tooth of Crime* so that you could step out of the play for a minute, every time a song comes, and be brought to an emotional comment on what's taking place in the play. When you go back to the play, you go back to the spoken word, then when a song comes again, it takes you out of it just a little bit. I wanted the music to be used as a kind of sounding-board for the play, you know."[23] While scouring London for musical inspiration for his plays, Shepard stumbled onto a distinctly British pastime that would alter his artistic ethos: dog racing, a sport that shows up in various ways in his writing from the early 1970s, especially in his plays *Blue Bitch* and *Geography of a Horse Dreamer,* the latter of which was Shepard's first attempt at directing. In his role as director, Shepard found that he had cleared up a lot of questions he had about his own writing. Directing *Geography,* he found a connection between his words and all the work done on their behalf. Specifically the young playwright found acting to be a window into writing; he would comment, "It's very like writing—you can't have any set kind of preconceptions about what it's going to be . . . because when you get to the actual thing it makes its own rules."[24]

Following the successful run of *Horse Dreamer* and the short plays *Little Ocean* and *Action,* Shepard, O-Lan, and Jesse packed up and headed back to the United States, only this time to California, the haunted land of Shepard's boyhood. There Shepard turned not to the adult excesses of rock 'n' roll and drugs that had inspired many of his works during the late 1960s and early 1970s, but to the familiar structure of the American family. Perhaps reminded of his own adolescence in California, Shepard wrote pieces in the mid to late 1970s that explored the mystery of the American family and how multiple identities—familial, sexual, gendered, and racial—were worked out within a highly competitive environment. Shepard and O-Lan eventually settled in Mill Valley, California, where the playwright set up his own twenty-acre ranch. It was as far away as a person might get from the urban excitement of London and New York, yet close enough that he could tap into the highly educated and liberal audiences of Berkeley and San Francisco. He found a home at the Magic Theatre in San Francisco and taught playwriting at the University of California at Davis. Back on familiar ground, Shepard began to write feverishly on his next set of plays—*Killer's Head, California Heart Attack,* and *Manfly* (a commissioned adaptation of Marlowe's *Doctor Faustus*)—until he was interrupted by a request from one of his biggest idols, Bob Dylan.

Dylan was planning to film a movie based loosely on his tour with the Rolling Thunder Revue, and he wanted to know if Shepard would come along to write key moments for the film. The film was to be a blend of fiction and documentary. The project appealed to the young Shepard, who was intrigued by the ideas such work might bring out in his plays. He had already been exploring rock 'n' roll, fiction, autobiography, and myth in his own work, and now Dylan was offering him a chance to collaborate beyond the stage. Shepard accepted the assignment. While on tour, Sam was struck by the ways Bob Dylan created his own mythology and the consequences of that creation: "Dylan says he's just a 'musician,' and in his boots he needs that kind of protection from intellectual probes, which are a constant threat to any artist. . . . Myth is a powerful medium because it talks to the emotions and not the head. It moves us into an area of mystery. Some myths are poisonous to believe in, but others have the capacity for changing something inside of us, even if it's just for a minute or two. Dylan creates a mythic atmosphere out of the land around us. The land we walk on every day and never see until someone shows it to us."[25] Though the movie that came from his time with Dylan (the enigmatic *Renaldo and Clara*) was a disappointment, Shepard was able to use his epiphany about myth and its relationships to character, atmosphere, and landscape in his next plays, *Angel City, The Sad Lament of Pecos Bill on the Eve of Killing His Wife,* and *Suicide in B-flat.* But Shepard's purposeful connection with mythology and his adolescence in California yielded a great success. Inspired by familial mythology, Shepard wrote *Curse of the Starving Class,* the first play in what is now known as his "family trilogy."

Curse of the Starving Class was different from Shepard's early plays in key ways. While his early works were short plays in one or two acts, Shepard designed *Curse* as a three-act exploration of the American family. He recognized the departure in subject matter as well: "*Curse* is the first time I've ever tried to deal with my family. Not really my family, just the—what do you call it—nuclear family. I've always been kind of scared of that. Because if you could really understand that, understand the chemistry and the reactions that are going on there, I've had the feeling you could understand a lot."[26] By going back to his family, Shepard felt he might understand core principles of his identity. During the writing of his new play, Shepard received constant inspiration in the form of short letters and brief visits from his father, who was beginning to write him letters "full of paternal pride and personal misery, asking for money and then apologizing for not writing sooner to express his gratitude. Drinking too much and eating too little, he'd hurt his elbow, got an infection, and couldn't afford to go to the doctor."[27] From these experiences, the characters and plot slowly took shape—Weston, the drunk and disappearing father who engages his family in power games; Ella, the ditzy and fading matriarch; Emma, the horse-obsessed tomboy dreamer; and Wesley, the protagonist who, in many ways, is a stand-in for Shepard himself as he attempts unsuccessfully to escape his father's influence and assert his own independence. One critic concluded that *Curse of the Starving Class* is a play whose "overall sweep . . . is tragic, taking in as it does the disintegration of the American family and the ascendency of a consumer society efficiently conditioned to value material goods over land and people."[28]

New York theater mogul Joseph Papp had commissioned *Curse of the Starving Class* for his Vivian Beaumont Theater, but the play first premiered in London at the Royal Court Theatre in 1977. The *Village Voice* presented Shepard with the 1977 Obie Award for Best New Play even though no one on staff had seen it. The play would eventually premiere in New York the following year at the Public Theater. After that production Shepard's life changed. Once regarded as a public figure—the enfant terrible of the off-off-Broadway movement, an auteur who wrote of his torrid affairs with rock stars and hobnobbed with Bob Dylan—Shepard quickly became a playwright of magnitude. *Curse of the Starving Class* declared to the literary world that Sam Shepard was an author capable of sustaining meanings beyond the transient ideas he explored in one-acts or rock 'n' roll plays. The play moved Shepard from his position as rock idol or popular gossip figure into the conversation with writers such as Tennessee Williams, Arthur Miller, and Eugene O'Neill.

While his play ran for a five-week stint in New York, Shepard worked as an actor in director Terrence Malick's critically lauded movie *Days of Heaven*. But his real interest continued to be writing, and he turned to his longtime friend Joe Chaikin to collaborate on a piece entitled *Tongues*. The piece was to be an experimental play revolving around what Chaikin called "a tale about somebody who might be reborn and reborn and reborn and reborn. . . . Sam likes egg foo yung, so we'd go to this Chinese restaurant, or we'd go to the park or to the zoo, or we'd stay in my hotel room. We would sit there and make something up. I'd sometimes make up a line, he'd follow it; he'd make up a line, I'd follow it."[29] Shepard's collaboration with Chaikin was a success; each man felt a kinship and mutual affection for the other's work. After *Tongue*'s successful run at the Magic Theatre, the pair teamed up again for *Savage/Love*. Chaikin described the new play as "common poems of real and imagined moments in the spell of love."[30] The collaboration helped mold Shepard's thoughts on writing, directing, and acting, and with Chaikin's techniques fresh in his mind, the playwright began his own workshop sessions with young actors at the Bay Area Playwrights Festival.

Shepard's next solo full-length play would pick up where the ideas of *Curse of the Starving Class* had left off. *Buried Child* can be read, in some ways, as a sequel to *Curse*, set six years down the road. Wesley has become Vince—still, in many ways, a stand-in for the playwright. He plans a visit to his grandparents' farm during a larger trip to his father's house in New Mexico. During his brief visit the family unravels emotionally until its members are forced to confront—quite literally—the skeletons in the closet. Shewey notes that the play is a "watershed play for Shepard. It's full of echoes from his previous works. . . . But *Buried Child* stands as a unique achievement . . . it is the control he exerts over the language and action of the play that gives its unorthodox effects such theatrical power."[31] The New York premiere of the play in 1979 drew rave reviews from audiences, but more important, it introduced Shepard to a wider critical audience. The day after it closed, Shepard received word that he had won the Pulitzer Prize for Drama, thus cementing the young playwright's status as one of America's greatest living artists.

The award opened up opportunities and audiences that Shepard had not considered possible just five years earlier, but he was not impressed with the trappings of his success: "I've been in a few rodeos, and the first team roping that I won gave me more of a feeling of accomplishment and pride of achievement than I ever got winning the Pulitzer Prize,"[32] he told an interviewer. Understandably Shepard felt increased pressure to produce a play that would live up to the magnitude of his new award, one that would confirm everyone's praise and commendations.

True West finishes Shepard's family trilogy by looking at two adult brothers, Austin and Lee, and their struggle to retain power—familial, authorial, intellectual, and physical—over each other. Shepard could not deny that his play had deep personal connections to his life: "I never intended [*True West*] to be a documentary of my personal life. It's always a mixture. But you can't get away from certain personal elements. I don't want to get away from certain personal elements that you use as hooks in a certain way. The further I get away from those personal things the more in the dark I am.

True West is riddled with personal sketches.[33] Biographer Don Shewey finds in Shepard's autobiographical sketches a larger meaning: "the notion that each man has to face the other side of himself, the person he might have been if he had (or hadn't) followed in his father's footsteps."[34] For Shepard the play came down to an exploration of "double nature. It's a real thing, double nature. I think we're split in a much more devastating way than psychology can ever reveal. It's not so cute."[35] The play premiered at the Magic Theatre in 1980 and then went onto a New York run at Joseph Papp's Public Theater. But it was the Steppenwolf Theatre in Chicago that gave *True West* its most meaningful production, with actor/director Gary Sinise playing the role of Austin and a little-known actor named John Malkovich as Lee.

Meanwhile Shepard was making a name for himself as a talented Hollywood actor. His turn in *Days of Heaven* led to a number of movie roles in films such as *Resurrection, Frances,* and *Raggedy Man.* He eventually landed a major role in the movie *The Right Stuff* as pilot Chuck Yeager, a performance that earned him an Academy Award nomination. That film propelled him to Hollywood stardom and would allow him to work as a professional actor for the rest of his life. Shepard was also becoming known as more than a writer of drama. In 1982 he published *Motel Chronicles,* his first collection of short fiction loosely based on real experiences. The collection persuaded Wim Wenders to collaborate with Shepard on a screenplay; the resulting film, *Paris, Texas,* would go on to win the Golden Palm award at the Cannes Film Festival. While he experienced great professional success as an actor, playwright, and fiction writer in the early 1980s, Shepard's personal life also underwent a tremendous change. During the filming of *Country* and *Crimes of the Heart,* Shepard began an intense love affair with costar Jessica Lange. Unlike his brief tryst with Patti Smith, Shepard and Lange's relationship endured. Eventually Shepard left O-Lan to move to New Mexico to be with Lange.

Based partly on his new, unstable relationship, Shepard began writing a play about a couple deeply in love who were nothing but trouble for each other. While *Fool for Love* can easily be seen as a reaction to his new love life, critics have cautioned against reading the play solely as a commentary on Lange and Shepard's relationship. Don Shewey has instead placed it as a natural corollary to *True West,* a play that explores double nature, "pitting man not against himself, but man against woman." Shepard, for his part, also steered clear of connecting the play with his new affair, claiming, "I was determined to write some kind of confrontation between a man and a woman, as opposed to just men. I wanted to try and take this leap into a female character, which I had never really done. I felt obliged to, somehow.

But it's hard for a man to say he can speak from the point of view of a woman. But you can make an attempt."[36] *Fool for Love* was well received by critics, and Shepard turned immediately from its success to familiar territory—another collaboration with friend Joseph Chaikin in *The War in Heaven*. It was during that collaboration, in the spring of 1984, that two major events occurred that would affect Shepard's life and art: the first was the death of his father in March 1984 following an automobile accident. The second event was Chaikin's heart attack and subsequent stroke that resulted in severe aphasia, affecting the writer's ability to speak coherently.

The dual blows deeply affected Shepard, and as he set about to write new work in May 1984, he conceived of a three-act play that explored what Shewey calls an "encapsulat[ion of] the previous four of Shepard's major plays, which themselves were an imaginative reflection of his own life story."[37] *A Lie of the Mind* examines the inner world of Jake, a rough man who beats his actress-wife Beth severely for dressing too promiscuously. What follows shows how Jake must deal with the emotional consequences of that attack from both his and Beth's family. Throughout the play, echoes of Shepard's life come through: "the breakup of his fourteen-year marriage when he left his wife, O-Lan, for Jessica Lange; his father's death in an auto accident; Chaikin's debilitating stroke," but these concerns become almost "self parody."[38] What were once a set of preoccupations with the inner turmoil of his family life begin to evolve into a self-aware (and sometimes consciously comedic) reflection on the ensuing melodrama.

Shepard directed the premiere of *A Lie of the Mind,* which opened with a celebrity cast that included Harvey Keitel, Amanda Plummer, Geraldine Page, and Rebecca de Mornay. Halfway through the process, Shepard decided he wanted to integrate music into the play, and sent for the North Carolina bluegrass band the Red Clay Ramblers. Despite the disturbing fact of the play revolving around the brutal beating of a woman, the premiere was a success and garnered Shepard excellent reviews. Shepard later explained that the play was, at its base, not literal, but explored "the female force in nature . . . [and] how that female thing relates to being a man. You know, in yourself, that the female part of one's self as a man is, for the most part, battered and beaten up and kicked to shit just like some women in relationships. That men themselves batter their own female part to their own detriment. And it became interesting from that angle—as a man, what is it like to embrace the female part of yourself that you historically damaged for one reason or another?"[39] Following both his critical success with the family trilogy and his Pulitzer Prize, Shepard signaled with *Fool for Love* and *A Lie of the Mind* that he had come a long way from the side-stages of the off-off-Broadway movement to the forefront of American theater.

After the success of *A Lie of the Mind,* Shepard disappeared from play-writing for several years; his focus shifted both to his newly growing family (his and Lange's daughter, Hannah, was born in 1986, and their son, Samuel Walker, was born in 1987) and acting. The family also moved from their homestead in Santa Fe to a farm in Scottsville, Virginia. Though Shepard appeared in some strange films in the late 1980s (1986's *Crimes of the Heart* was followed by the 1987 screwball comedy *Baby Boom,* which, in turn, was followed by the 1989 melodrama *Steel Magnolias*), he became a recognizable figure in America cinema, often portraying the font of mature and untamed masculine sexuality.

In 1987, during a break in his acting, Shepard wrote a screenplay for Lange, which he also planned to direct. *Far North* followed the story of a young woman, named Kate, who comes back to her father's home to look after him following an injury he sustains with a wild horse. Shepard was hesitant to call his screenplay a "feminist piece," but he acknowledged that his work during this time period followed the force of the feminine even within the realm of masculinity: "the women suddenly took on a different light than they had before. Because before it felt so sort of overwhelmed by the confusion about masculinity . . . that sort of overwhelmed the female." He followed *Far North* with the 1993 movie *Silent Tongue.* If *Far North* was Shepard's cinematic meditation on the strength and resiliency of women, *Silent Tongue* was his exploration of the bonds between men, especially fathers and sons. However, both movies were critical and popular failures, and they would all but end Shepard's careers as screenwriter and film director.

Frustrated with the world of cinema, Shepard turned back to his first love, the stage. In the 1990s Shepard wrote three major plays, *States of Shock, Simpatico,* and *Eyes for Consuela.* In the first, Shepard appears to go back to his early plays, where he experimented with language, character, and music. The play has the feel of a quickly written, frenetic experiment that, Shepard claims, is a response to the Gulf War. Shepard would later comment on the central character of the colonel in *States of Shock,*

> I was in Kentucky when the war opened. I was in a bar that I go to a lot down there because it's a horseman's bar. Normally that bar is just a din of conversation and people having a great time and talking about horses and this, that, and the other. And I walked in the bar and it was stone silence. The TV was on, and these planes were coming in, and suddenly . . . it

just seemed like doomsday to me. I could not believe the systematic kind of insensitivity of it. That there was this punitive attitude—we're going to just knock these people off the face of the earth. And then it's devastating. Not only that, but they've convinced the American public that this was a good deed, that this was in fact a heroic fucking war, and welcome the heroes back. What fucking heroes, man?. . . The notion of this being a heroic event is just outrageous. . . . . I just got so outraged by the whole hoax of it, and the way everything is choked down and censored in the media. . . . I wanted to create a character of such outrageous, repulsive, military, fascist demonism that the audience would recognize it and say, "Oh, this is the essence of this thing."[40]

The play opened in 1993, but it was not the critical darling that *A Lie of the Mind* or *Fool for Love* had been. Many saw Shepard going backward to old habits and preoccupations instead of moving forward to new territory.

Later in the fall of that year, Shepard finished a new three-act play, *Simpatico*. This new play took as its subject the world of horse racing, but it also explored Shepard's obsession with the dual nature of man. Like Austin and Lee in *True West,* the main characters of *Simpatico* are polar opposites: Carter is the well-to-do manager who cannot escape his past with his partner Vinnie, a deadbeat and drunk. Critics compared *Simpatico* to the travesty of *States of Shock;* many roundly criticized both for the return to an experimental aesthetic and detached voice. One critic described the play this way: "The plot is ludicrous and inconsequential. The characters do wacky things with no apparent logical motivation. They sustain an easy and sometimes lively banter, but the dialogue latches onto actions that propel the play from scene to scene."[41] Though the play "contains traces of Shepard's familiar fixations," they do not, ultimately, lead to "any new directions."[42]

Despite the disappointment of his two plays in the early 1990s, Shepard was happy to see the fruition of his collaboration with Chaikin on *The War in Heaven.* The play that they had first talked about in 1981 was finally performed by Chaikin in 1991, even though his stroke had made speaking difficult. The result of that collaboration spurred the friends to work again, this time on a play entitled *When the World Was Green,* a piece again with two characters: a murderer who is waiting to be executed and the inquisitive, young reporter who comes to find the story behind the crime. The play was commissioned for the 1996 Olympics and had its premiere during the festival at Seven Stages in Atlanta.

Though Shepard did not write many plays during the late 1990s, his career as an American legend was cemented by a new book of fiction and by numerous revivals of his old plays (including the first Shepard play ever to appear on Broadway, the revival of *Buried Child*). Audiences were exposed to many of his plays produced in the 1960s and 1970s for the first time, and a new generation of critics, scholars, and audiences saw the trajectory of a career that was full of energy, rhythm, and mythology. New productions of old scripts gave life to works that had not been performed in ten or fifteen years.

In the last ten years, Shepard has continued to produce plays while balancing his life as an actor and intellectual. In 2000 he premiered *The Late Henry Moss* and, soon after, wrote *The God of Hell,* which, in some ways, is Shepard's reaction to the vitriol embedded within the patriotism expressed after September 11, 2001. His 2007 play, *Kicking a Dead Horse,* is almost an entire play sustained by the monologue of a man alone onstage trying to understand his life and how he might move beyond his limitations. And, finally, his 2009 play, *Ages of the Moon,* opened to critical success in both Dublin and New York and continues the ethos he first established in early plays such as *La Turista*. Shepard produced these plays despite acting in many movies and finishing several short story collections.

Throughout his life Shepard has not been afraid to explore the demons of his childhood, his adolescence, and his love life; all these stories that make up the man resonate in the world of the playwright. But it is his passion for tearing down the walls that separate man from his true identity that has struck such a chord with audiences and scholars. Understanding Sam Shepard's life is critical to understanding Sam Shepard's work, and in the pages that follow, the careful reader will find echoes of Shepard's life buried within his words.

CHAPTER 2

Experimentations with Sound, Language, and Myth
The Early Plays, 1964–1976

When Shepard burst onto the New York City theater scene in the middle of the 1960s, audiences did not quite know what to make of his plays. Blending the language of poetry, performance art, rock 'n' roll lyrics, and mythology, Shepard's first plays seemed completely different from most dramas routinely appearing on American stages. As a writer, Shepard found himself drawn to performance pieces because they "happened in three dimensions . . . that came to life in space rather than in a book."[1] The experience of watching a play was interactive and collaborative, and the young Sam Shepard explored that engagement between characters and audience in his earliest plays. Seeing a Sam Shepard play was an experience, one shared between audience and actors. It was difficult to watch Shepard's early pieces and not be affected: in them he often went out of his way—with long, unbroken monologues, quick, random action, and an emphasis on the violent, bizarre and grotesque—to make the audience uncomfortable. To all who witnessed these early Sam Shepard plays, it was clear that the new playwright was attempting something unusual.

Though audiences found his distinctive, dramatic voice to be uncompromisingly original, Shepard ascribed his engaging style not to a purposeful authorial voice, but rather to his complete lack of experience: "I didn't really have any references for the theatre, except for the few plays that I'd acted in. But in a way I think that was better for me, because I didn't have any idea how to shape an action into what is seen—so the so-called originality of the early work just comes from ignorance. I just didn't know."[2] The playwright's early works fell between Samuel Beckett's theater of the absurd and Bertolt Brecht's concept of character. However, Shepard is quick to note that the Brecht is "my favorite playwright."[3] One can sense Brecht's presence in the early career of Shepard, for it is Brecht who "developed the concept of character as situated between the actor (I) and the role (you). Character created from the point of view of the third person (he), from the outside event: narrative acting." Shepard revised the Brechtian model of character "by situating narration in the present, in the equation of character as narrator, and so eliminating gestus in favor of the tone of voice. He substitutes myth for history, experience for theory."[4] In his early plays Shepard created characters who comment on events happening onstage in real time, as though collapsing the notion of time and history altogether. Similarly Shepard experimented with language and sound, employing techniques similar to those of Brecht's "musicals" such as *Mahagonny* and *The Threepenny Opera.*

In many of Shepard's earliest pieces, one can also see the playwright's debt to Samuel Beckett. In *Cowboys,* for example, two protagonists pass their time in pointless banter about events that never seem to happen; the (in)action onstage parallels the lack of meaningful dialogue between Beckett's Vladimir and Estragon in *Waiting for Godot.* Seemingly insignificant events take on great importance, and much of the "action" of both Shepard's early pieces and Beckett's oeuvre take places inside the mind of the characters onstage. Shepard was not the only playwright to be influenced by Beckett, and he references many of the progeny of the great absurdist dramatist in his early work as well: *4-H Club* (1964) recalls the frantic absurdity of Edward Albee's *The Sandbox,* while *Red Cross* (1966) has echoes of Harold Pinter's language play.

Rather than attempting to imitate Brecht, Beckett, Albee, Pinter, or the other artists of the absurdist movement, Shepard took the theater of the absurd aesthetic as his starting point to experiment with language, character, and action. But Shepard's interest was not simply formal and academic; Bottoms has noted that he used "sources as diverse as movie westerns (the cowboys-and-Indians role-play) and high school science lessons or gym classes."[5] Shepard mixed levels of discourse in order to manifest their artificiality and point out ridiculous connections. Frequently characters speak to one another outside the action onstage, and their language is marked by fragments and images that sometimes contradict one another. Characters may recite long monologues about inconsequential matters, like what they ate for dinner or the importance of cleanliness, but nothing ever comes of these long soliloquies. Perhaps what Shepard's earliest plays have in common with one another is the emphasis on the fragment itself, either in word or image.

The One-Acts (1964–1967)

In 1964 Shepard's two first-performed plays, *Cowboys* and *The Rock Garden,* appeared at a small venue off-off-Broadway called Theatre Genesis. Shepard would eventually rework *Cowboys* into another play, but the ethos of the piece remained the same: it explored the freedom and fear of being a young man encountering a new frontier. *The Rock Garden,* however, was much more personal. Shepard described it as being about "leaving my mom and dad. It happens in two scenes. In the first scene the mother is lying in bed ill while the son is sitting in a chair, and she is talking about this special sort of cookie that she makes, which is marshmallow on salt crackers melted under the oven. It's called angels on horseback, and she has a monologue about it. And then the father arrives in the second scene. The boy doesn't say anything, . . . and the father starts to talk about painting the fence around the house, and there's a monologue about that. . . . Finally the boy has a monologue about orgasm that goes on for a couple of pages and ends in him coming all over the place. . . . The father also talks about this rock garden, which is his obsession, a garden where he collects all these rocks from different sojourns to the desert."[6]

As his earliest plays, *Cowboys* and *The Rock Garden* establish several trajectories that Sam Shepard would explore more deeply in his later work; *The Rock Garden,* for example, investigates the question of identity, especially the tricky subject of familial identity. Both plays are curious about the possibility for reinventing one's identity, a topic that would have especially interested the young playwright who was attempting to "create a new identity for himself" in New York by getting "as far away as possible from his family home in California."[7] Surrounded by the dull droning of his mother and father, the "boy" in *The Rock Garden* appears static, restrained, and lifeless. Several times during his father's monologue, he actually falls asleep. It is only when he celebrates his identity through his assertion of a newfound sexual power that he becomes active and alive, and it is exactly at that moment that his father becomes dormant and lame: as he completes his graphic monologue, the boy fails to notice that his old man has fallen out of his chair and onto the floor.

After writing the two one-acts, Shepard went through the most prolific period of his life. Between 1964 and 1967, Shepard wrote ten plays that were performed in front of enthusiastic audiences in New York City. However, not all his plays were as successful and engaging as *The Rock Garden*. Shepard has described *Up to Thursday* as simply a "bad exercise in absurdity I guess. This kid is sleeping in an American flag, he's only wearing a jockstrap or something, and there's four people on stage who keep shifting their legs and talking. I can't remember it very well—it's only been done once. It was a terrible play."[8]

The next two plays, *Dog* and *Rocking Chair*, were also similarly forgettable. If *Up to Thursday* was a riff on Samuel Beckett's *Endgame*, Shepard recalls *Dog* as a failed attempt to imitate Albee: "*Dog* was about a black guy—which I later found out it was uncool for a white to write about in America. It was about a black guy on a park bench, a sort of *Zoo-Story* type play. I don't even remember *Rocking Chair*, except it was about somebody in a rocking chair."[9] Weighed down with heavy-handed symbolism and trying to mimic the plays that came before them, Shepard's first five plays only hinted at the work that was to come. But though Shepard remembers his earliest work as derivative and sophomoric, the plays' ethos of experimentation would eventually serve the young playwright well in his next endeavors.

Each one-act that followed *Cowboys* and *The Rock Garden* started with an image. Shepard would take these abstract pictures and use them as the tableau that starts the action of the play. Shepard found that his emphasis on image first encompassed the beauty of theater itself: "When you talk about images, an image can be seen without looking at anything—you can see something in your head, or you can see something on stage, or you can see things that don't appear on stage, you know. The fantastic thing about theatre is that it can make something be seen that's invisible, and that's where my interest in theatre is—that you can be watching this thing happening with actors and costumes and light and set and language, and even plot, and something emerges from beyond that, and that's the image part that I'm looking for, that's the sort of added dimension."[10] Each initial tableau does the work of establishing the unchanging parts of Shepard's one-act: setting, character, and tone. The only variable that shifts throughout the performance is the characters' dialogue and action, though both are often repeated throughout.

His play *4-H Club* opens on "an empty stage except for a small kitchen upstage left . . . The floor of the kitchen is littered with paper, cans, and various trash . . . The walls are very dirty . . . JOHN is downstage facing the audience kneeling beside the hot plate. He is stirring something in the pot with a spoon. BOB stands in the middle of the kitchen jumping up and down and laughing wildly. JOE stands upstage beside the door with a broom. He is hitting the door with the broom and laughing with BOB."[11] Besides establishing the abject poverty of the characters, Shepard's stage directions reveal each character's personality. While the stakes of the scene shift and change, the fundamental relationship among the characters does not: Joe obsesses over the cleanliness and tidiness of the trashed space, while John is focused solely on his own wants and needs. Buried within the play is another staple of the early Shepard piece: the long, dramatic monologue. Attempting to tell his friends about the importance of cleanliness, Joe begins to recite a memory from his youth where he was employed as a driveway sweeper. Like many of Shepard's extended monologues, Joe's revels in the details of his memories and speaks reverently of his past experiences. Bottoms has compared these long monologues to a "solo jazz break" because "each speech contains its own internal dynamic of shifting tempos, crescendos, and diminuendos."[12]

4-H Club explores a variety of themes—poverty, hunger, paranoia, fear, uncertainty—but it does so with a dreamy, comic tone. The three characters could be the Three Stooges for all of their pratfalls and deliberately banal dialogue. During the course of the play, the men dream of food and companionship, of their youth and honest work, of going back to a simpler time. They imagine the possibility of starting a riot only by throwing apples, and in their imagination, the potential revolution brings down the entire federal government. But the men are not revolutionaries; they are comic figures. The play ends with each man attempting to stomp to death giant, invisible mice that have somehow invaded their apartment. In 4-H Club, Shepard appears to be poking fun at the naive idealism of the 1960s counterculture, while simultaneously expressing an earnest admiration for the sense of community behind it. Joe, Bob, and John all dream of leaving their dull existence, but, like Beckett's Vladimir and Estragon, they are powerless to change their surroundings. The play ends with John telling the others that he is leaving on a vacation. Promising to send postcards, he never leaves but continues to explain to them how nice it will be to swim "floating on my back. You just float and stare at the sky. You just float and stare at the sky. You just float and stare at the sky."[13] Nothing happens in 4-H Club. The men end the play in roughly the same positions as they began it. And while they address some heady issues, they come to no conclusions and offer one another only illusions of escape. 4-H Club is indicative of a series of early Shepard one-acts, such as Icarus's Mother (1965), Chicago (1965), Fourteen Hundred Thousand (1966), and Red Cross (1966). But by 1967 Shepard began to conceive of a play that would explore more complicated issues, and therefore, he needed more time.

La Turista (1967)

Like the plays that preceded it, *La Turista* was modeled on a specific memory from Shepard's past: this time a terrible night spent in Mexico with his then girlfriend Joyce Aaron. From that memory, the play took shape: initially Shepard wrote the play in three acts, but Jacques Levy, the director, was unhappy with the progression of the play after the first act. Instead of rewriting the second and third acts, Shepard essentially combined the two into a new second act and presented it as his completed project. The result becomes what one critic calls, "an intriguing juxtaposition of two radically different halves."[14]

In the first act the setting is a dazzling, bright hotel room in Mexico where an American couple, Salem and Kent (named humorously after two brands of cigarettes), sit in their underwear cooling off their sunburned bodies underneath the fan in their room. Kent suffers from a severe case of dysentery, which causes him to run to the bathroom frequently. During his sickness, a young boy enters the room asking to shine the couple's shoes. When the two try to shoo him away, the boy spits on Kent and takes his place on his bed; disgusted, Kent retreats to clean himself in the bathroom. When the man returns, he faints at the sight of the filthy boy defiling his bed. The woman calls down for a doctor. As Salem also suffers from diarrhea in the bathroom, she is oblivious to the entrance of a Mexican witch doctor who performs a ritual cleansing of Kent with the aid of blood from two chickens that he kills onstage. When Salem comes out of the bathroom, she dons a poncho and heads into the audience to try to sell the boy. They are interrupted by a phone call from the boy's father, who has asked his son to come back home.

The second act is the mirror image of the first: now Kent and Salem sit in a bland, tan room of an American hotel. Salem has again called a doctor to treat her husband, who now suffers from a more inexplicable "soul sickness," whose only physical symptom is constant laziness. When the doctor and his son arrive, they are dressed in Civil War regalia. The doctor treats Kent with a mixture of old-fashioned medicine and forced physical activity. When Kent eventually reawakens, he challenges the doctor's authority by inventing a competing narrative to counter the stories the doctor and his son have been telling. Kent becomes increasingly agitated, and when Salem, the doctor, and his son try to corner Kent to treat him more extensively, the man runs through the back wall, leaving behind a hole shaped like his fleeing body.

Like Shepard's early one-acts, *La Turista* uses long, dramatic monologues in key places, but the end of the play conceives of a dual narration that challenges the single voice found in plays such as *4-H Club*. The doctor and his son try to take control of Kent and Salem, but the man thwarts their attempts by wresting narrative control away from them. He imagines his own story—ironically, about a doctor who invents a terrible beast beyond his control—that gradually overtakes the story the doctor has been telling. This cross narration might represent Shepard's revision of himself and his reliance on the dramatic monologue as a narrative technique. Kent collapses the importance of the doctor's narrative by reimagining his stories, and he shifts the focus away from the linear narrative of the boy and his father and into a fantastical, science fiction narrative that recalls *Frankenstein*.

La Turista also renegotiates the boundaries of the stage by having the characters acknowledge members of the audience during climactic moments. In act 1 the boy sits downstage center and stares into the seats of the theater "mak[ing] different monster faces at the audience, from sticking his tongue out to giving them the finger."[15] By the end of the act, Salem transforms herself into a version of a Mexican peasant and takes the boy "by the hand and leads him downstage center; she leads him back and forth by the hand downstage and speaks to the audience as though it were a market place full of villagers."[16] Eventually she leaves the stage entirely and goes "into the audience . . . up and down the aisles showing the BOY to the people and yelling loudly." The action does not end at the apron of the stage but extends into the audience itself. Shepard, in his self-effacing humor, comments through this unique device on the "illusion" the play creates for the members of an audience who, regardless of interest, are cast as an unwitting mass being duped by Salem.

But Shepard's most sustained meditation in *La Turista* involves the mind/body split as it is manifest through the different cultural responses to medicine. In both acts Kent suffers from a sickness. In act 1 he complains of diarrhea, vomiting, and abdominal cramps, all symptoms associated with "Montezuma's revenge," a slang term that denotes a traveler's diarrhea, especially one caught by tourists visiting Mexico. Kent believes his affliction to be a test of his manhood, and he asserts that his passing through it means he has passed a crucial test: "Yes, sir! Nothing like a little amoebic dysentery to build up a man's immunity to his environment. That's the trouble with the States you know. Everything's so clean and pure and immaculate up there that a man doesn't even have a chance to build up his own immunity."[17] In the course of his self-congratulations, however, Kent notes the Mexican boy has infiltrated his bed, and, in a humorous commentary on his imagined masculinity, he immediately faints. Though he is able to overcome (and even celebrate) the stomach affliction he contracts in a foreign land, Kent cannot bide the potential for infestation and sickness the exotic boy represents. His sickness is not so much physical as it is an internal, a malaise arising from his middle-class, suburban, white perspective, a perspective Shepard eviscerates throughout act 1.

After Kent faints, he is attended to by a witch doctor who arrives to perform a ritual over his body meant to cleanse the bad spirits and invite good ones inside his body. The boy confesses, however, much to Salem's horror, that the ritual has killed Kent. Moreover he concludes, "He's dead. . . . You're both dead."[18] However, the declaration is not a diagnosis, but an assertion of the impotence of Salem and Kent's domesticated perspective. In act 2 Kent suffers from a more indefinable sickness, one that presents without physical symptoms. To the American doctor, such a sickness is unfathomable, and he has no way to treat it: "Tell me somethin'," he asks Salem, "Somethin'. Gotta go on somethin' when you're treatin' illness. Otherwise you might as well be treatin' health."[19] But the sickness does not present with physical symptoms, and therefore, Kent does not respond to the doctor's Western cures.

Shepard's ending suggests that Kent's sickness is connected with a desire to escape, to flee, to be on his own; he has lived, in essence, as a tourist in his own body. His journey to self-discovery necessitates a daring escape. At the end of the play, the man makes a grand exit: he grabs a rope "and swings over [Salem and Sonny's] heads. He lands on the ramp behind DOC and runs straight toward the upstage wall of the set and leaps right through it, leaving a cut-out silhouette of his body in the wall."[20] Perhaps the only cure for Kent lies in his ability to venture outside his surroundings and experience other lives and cultures—not as a closeted tourist, who views the indigenous people as potential scam artists and sources of disease—but as a fellow traveler, like the misunderstood beast he speaks of in his narrative. By escaping the circuitous logic of Western culture, Kent establishes the potential to cure himself of his soul sickness through the absence of his body. Shepard further emphasizes that absence by having the lights dim on the silhouette of Kent's body as he crashes through the wall and into the night.

Sex, Drugs, and Rock 'n' Roll, 1967–1971

Though he made his name as a playwright, Shepard's initial love was music. From early adolescence, he envisioned himself as a rock 'n' roll star. At the beginning of his career, in 1964, America was being overtaken by the music of a young generation: the British invasion was in full swing, and the beginnings of the counterculture were expressed through the protest songs of Bob Dylan and the noisy, visceral guitar of Jimmy Hendrix. Shepard internalized the disparate musical scenes that were influencing popular culture and used them in his plays. From 1968 to 1972, many of Shepard's plays included music as either another textual element or a distinct narrative subplot. Shepard himself appeared onstage in several bands at the time. His most famous collaborative partners were with the band Holy Modal Rounders, who would appear in several of Shepard's works during the late 1960s.

Shepard's first play that deals directly with the world of rock 'n' roll is *Melodrama Play* (1967). In it Shepard envisioned a band performing alongside the actors and, in an extreme stage direction, counseled future directors to "have the band suspended from the ceiling in a cage over the audience's head."[21] The play opens on a room adorned with posters of "Bob Dylan . . . [and] an equally large photo of Robert Goulet without eyes"[22] and takes as its subject songwriter Duke Durgens, who is trying to compete with himself. He has created a number-one hit record, but cannot seem to follow up the success of his first recording. As his first rock 'n' roll play, Shepard's *Melodrama Play* explores questions of authorship, "selling out," and the power of music to incite revolution, but critics found the piece "only interesting really as a warm-up for later plays"[23] such as *Geography of a Horse Dreamer* (1974) and *The Tooth of Crime* (1972).

In his next play, *Forensic and the Navigators* (1967), Shepard envisioned two radical revolutionaries, Emmet and Forensic, both of whom are militant about attacking the dominant culture. When the character of Oolan (written specifically for O-Lan, Shepard's wife at the time) offers pancakes to them, Emmet explodes, "How many times I gotta tell you I don't eat that buck-wheat Aunt Jemima middle-class bullshit."[24] The two are targeted by agents (it is unclear who sent them or why) who arrive to gas them, but briefly Forensic and Emmet get the upper hand. They attempt to trade Oolan for secrets from the agents: where did the men come from and how did they know how to attack their home base? But the play ends with smoke and gas seeping onstage. As in Shepard's early one-acts, there are several sustained monologues in the play, but the juxtaposition of music and action is most striking. Shewey has noted that, at the end of the performances, "colored smoke started filling up the theater until the stage was invisible" (60). While the smoke pours out, the band the Moray Eels "came on and started to play very loudly, literally driving the audience from the theater."[25]

Though Shepard continued to collaborate with word and text in plays such as *Operation Sidewinder* (1970), *The Holy Ghostly* (1969), and *Shaved Splits* (1970), his exploration of the rock 'n' roll aesthetic is clearest in his complex piece *The Unseen Hand* (1969). The main character of his play is an old outlaw with a guitar, Blue Morphan, who is dressed in the guise of a rock 'n' roll musician: cowboy boots, overcoat, and a scraggily beard. The plot is complicated but involves intergalactic space travel, a debate over resistance to the dominant American suburban culture, and the power of the mind to escape the mundane everydayness of life. Blue Morphan might be a homeless drifter living on the side of the highway in a broken-down car, but to Willie, a "space freak" who has traveled into the past to ask for his help, he represents salvation from the punishing world of "the sorcerers of the High Commission."[26] The play suggests that Blue Morphan's pseudo-outlaw/ rock 'n' roll persona has the potential to eradicate the bonds of oppression; to Willie he represents a relic from the past, the Old West cowboy who can bring truth and justice back to the higher powers that attempt to destroy free thought. Unlike the pieces that came before it, *The Unseen Hand* offers the clearest example of Shepard's vision of rock 'n' roll music and its power to heal.

The Tooth of Crime (1972)

Though he explored the visceral and curative power of rock 'n' roll music in many plays before it, Sam Shepard's thoughts on the collaboration between music and text came to a culmination in *The Tooth of Crime*. In addition to its experimentation with music (the play, like those before it, calls for a live band to play onstage with the action), *The Tooth of Crime* also plays with the language of music, youth culture, and the idioms of rock 'n' roll. The main character, Hoss, opens the play singing lyrics that—in the style of rock 'n' roll bands from the 1970s—are poetic, mystifying, and highly allusive. As the play continues, Hoss's dialogue with other characters (especially between him and his "management") also mimics the prosaic and visceral lyrics of rock 'n' roll. When the rock n' roll star Crow appears to challenge Hoss's style, his dialogue is nearly incomprehensible to both the audience and Hoss: it mixes 1950s slang, British idioms, and references to youth culture from multiple decades.

The play reimagines the rock 'n' roll scene as a mixture of point-grubbing professional sports teams and ever escalating competitions between rival gangs. Each performer in the world of *The Tooth of Crime* is anxious to lock down a certain territory that awards him a number of points, and the winner of the most points receives the elusive gold record. The main character, Hoss, is clearly the next "big thing." He owns points that represent much of the West Coast (including the prize of California), and while other individuals have a following, Hoss is ahead in the points standings. Still he is unsure of himself and his place in "the game." He has become bored with success and worries that fame has domesticated him. Hoss is further shaken when he learns that a new performer, a "gypsy" who plays outside the rules of the game, is on the way to challenge his supremacy. With heroin and cocaine from a "doctor" and a pep talk from his girlfriend/groupie/manager, Becky Lou, he prepares for a battle with the newcomer.

When Crow arrives in act 2, he takes his place in the only set piece, Hoss's throne that sits in the middle of the stage. As the two characters interact, Hoss becomes more and more nervous at Crow's language and style. He had initially assumed the rock star to be an unseasoned kid, but he is shocked to learn that Crow has a style that appears to be uniquely his own. With the help of a referee, Hoss and Crow engage in a confusing match that resembles everything from a basketball game to a boxing match. Somehow the referee calls the match for Crow, and in a rage Hoss shoots the official dead. Stung by his defeat, Hoss offers all his territory in exchange for Crow's teaching him the "new style" Crow seems to possess so effortlessly. Unable to learn new moves, however, Hoss concludes that his rock persona has all been a lie, and in a final moment onstage, he performs what he considers the most individualistic and free act of his career: he shoots himself in the head. Without Hoss in his way, Crow begins a new journey as the next big thing with Hoss's ex-girlfriend, Becky Lou, by his side.

Embedded within the play is a meditation on the slipperiness of fame and how it bifurcates identity into public and private personas. Like the play that preceded it, *Cowboy Mouth* (1971), *The Tooth of Crime* acknowledges the illusory nature of public personas and their destructive effect on one's self-perception. Hoss has built up a following with his persona as an individualistic and ruthless performer; with the help of his driver, Cheyenne, and his manager, Becky Lou, he has amassed a great deal of territory and fame. But the experience has left him domesticated and neutered. He began his journey as a "killer" but now is forced to play a "game" that he no longer understands. As the action unfolds, it is hard not to find similarities between Hoss and Shepard—two public figures working out guilt over their fame and anxious over their artistic integrity. In a scene that has obvious connections to Shepard's anxiety over his own public persona, Hoss tells Cheyenne, "Can't you see what's happened to us. We ain't Markers no more. We ain't even Rockers. We're punk chumps cowering under the Keepers and the Refs and the critics and the public eye. We ain't free no more! Goddamnit! We ain't flyin' in the eye of contempt. We've become respectable and safe. Soft, mushy chewable ass lickers. What's happened to our killer heart. What's happened to our blind fucking courage! . . . We were warriors once."[27] All the reasons that Hoss decided to become a performer have been robbed of their meaning. "There's no sense of tradition in the game no more. There's no game," he laments to himself.[28] In a moment that recalls Kent's desire to escape in *La Turista,* Hoss dreams of escaping his fame and public identity and moving out into the country, living anonymously and becoming a nobody. "What about the country," he asks Becky Lou, "Ain't there any farmers left, ranchers, cowboys, open space? Nobody just livin' their life."[29] Hoss is no longer satisfied with the supposed "freedom" of being a rock star; "I just wanna have some fun," he confides to Becky.

During this crisis of identity, Hoss comes face to face with Crow, who represents something of a style chameleon. Though he speaks in the language of the gypsies, Crow embodies the mysterious shifting nature of popular culture itself. The language Crow speaks has an even more mystifying sound than Hoss's; Crow's speech deliberately exudes hidden meanings. Hoss cannot, at first, decipher Crow, but he learns quickly that the language means nothing: it simply voices a persona the performer has adopted to appear mysterious and cool. When Crow slips into "normal" speech patterns, Hoss pounces: "There! Why'd you slip just then? Why'd you suddenly talk like a person? You're into a wider scope than I thought. You're playin' my time, Gypsy but it ain't gonna work."[30]

Still in the world of the "game," where style trumps substance, Hoss can no longer keep up. During their intense duel in act 2, Hoss moves in and out of various speech patterns, from a "cowboy-Western image" ("I reckon you ain't never even seen a knife. A pup like you") to a "1920s gangster style" ("You mugs expect to horn in on our district and not have to pay da' price?") and finally to a racialized voodoo priest who chides Crow for his lack of roots ("Yo' music's in yo' head. You a blind minstrel with a phoney shuffle.").[31] But despite slightly wounding Crow's confidence, Hoss enters the third round in a draw because the referee cannot understand the importance of the rhythm-and-blues origins of rock 'n' roll. The game has become about the next new thing, not the tradition.

When Crow wins the "battle," Hoss believes he can still continue with his life as a rock star. "I'll develop my own image. I'm an original man. A one and only," he tells Crow,[32] but he immediately doubts his potential to sustain a single identity. He asks Crow to teach him how to be like him, but those attempts also fail. In one final attempt, Hoss creates an identity for himself that, even by the end of his monologue, he knows is baseless, born of cliché and meaningless phrases, and, more important, wholly disconnected from his private identity: "Mean and tough and cool. Untouchable. A true killer. Don't take no shit from nobody. True to his heart. True to his voice.

Everything's whole and unshakeable. His eyes cut through the jive. He knows his own fate. Beyond doubt. True courage in every move. Trusts every action to be what it is. Knows where he stands. Lives by a code. His own code. . . . Pitiless. Indifferent and riding a state of grace. It ain't me! IT AIN'T ME! IT AIN'T ME! IT AIN'T ME!"[33] In the end it is Hoss's recognition of the difference between the two identities—the performer and the person—that causes him to give up his hope of being a famous rock star. Unlike Crow, who in his song sings "I believe in my mask—The man I made up is me,"[34] Hoss cannot accept the invented persona that keeps him relevant in the industry. Rather than giving in to the meaninglessness of the disguise, he takes his own life.

By the end of the play, the audience recognizes Shepard's cynical exploration of stardom and fame as a commentary on his own tortured experience as a famous figure of American popular culture. As an off-off-Broadway sensation, the next big thing in the American stage, and a tabloid sensation due to his affair with Patti Smith, Shepard's struggles mirror Hoss's; both author and character share an anxiety over the consequences of fame. Like Hoss, Shepard must have feared that his original style would be co-opted by other playwrights, who would, in turn, sanitize them for mass consumption. Though Hoss loses his life at the end of the play, he goes down a hero. Crow calls him a "genius," and Becky Lou admits, "He was . . . one a' the great ones."[35] However, even though the play ends with a celebration of Hoss's integrity, the knowledge that his final act—suicide—represents the truest mark of originality in a world of meaningless style haunts any victory Hoss might have won.

"THERE'S VOICES COMING AT ME!": Shepard and His Craft, 1974–1976

After *Tooth of Crime*, Shepard's next five plays—*Geography of a Horse Dreamer* (1974), *Action* (1974), *Killer's Head* (1975), *Angel City* (1976), and *Suicide in B Flat* (1976)—can be read as allegories that investigate the playwright's crafting of stories. Shepard hinted at his interest in documenting the work of an artist through the character of Hoss, who, like Shepard, became a famous artist anxious about his notoriety and public persona. In *Geography of a Horse Dreamer,* the artist Shepard explores is Cody, a young man with the ability to see the winners of horse races in his dreams. Once his talent makes him famous, Cody is kidnapped from his Wyoming town and forced to supply the mobster Fingers and his cronies with the names of winning horses in upcoming races. Unlike Hoss, who has some control over his art and its consequences, Cody is completely cut off from the rest of the world. The mobsters keep him tied up and blindfolded in cheap hotel rooms. However, Cody shares a few similarities with Hoss: like the rock 'n' roll star, Cody has been exploited by those who wish to make a profit from his talent; both also see their talent as a burden. Shepard also connected Cody's talent with the mystery of music. One of the only possessions that Cody is allowed to keep after being kidnapped is a busted-up record of zydeco musician Clifton Chenier. The record helps the young man with his choices. He explains, "In the beginning I came up with six fifteen-to-one shots in a row. Six of 'em. And all of 'em came from the music. It's a source of inspiration."[36]

Also like Hoss, Cody pines for the wide open spaces of the prairie, where he can live free and alone. He tells his gangster-kidnappers that all he wants is to "go back to Wyoming and raise sheep . . . I'm from the Great Plains not the city."[37] Being trapped in hotel rooms in urban centers, Cody becomes a zombie; he cannot practice his art with any skill. He needs open spaces and clean air to do his art. These obvious parallels between Hoss and Cody reflect parallels to the artist himself. Shepard, who, at the time, was living with O-Lan in London, began to feel dissatisfied with the world surrounding him. Questioning his commitment to a craft that took so much out of him, Shepard longed to escape into the country again. His reputation as a cowboy rock star—largely fueled by his affair with Patti Smith and their tabloid spectacle *Cowboy Mouth*—followed him to England, but he was unable to shake the feeling that his persona was eclipsing his talent.

His anxiety over his persona as well as his experimentation with music are articulated further in *Suicide in B-flat*, a play that explores the nature of art, myth, and heroes. Like many of Shepard's early plays, *Suicide in B-flat* operates on two levels, with both a literal and a figurative plot. The main action of the play recalls a film-noir plot as two detectives attempt to piece together the supposed suicide of Niles, a well-known musician whose body has been discovered with its face blown off. But the symbolic narrative of the play investigates the demands of art on the artist. We learn that Niles did not kill himself but rather staged the scene in order to escape his growing fame. Niles appears several times onstage with Paulette, a dream figure who may or may not exist and who helps him ritualistically murder various parts of his persona, including, in a nod to Shepard's plays of the past, a cowboy.

In piecing together the supposed "crime," the two detectives attempt to create a narrative for Niles's growing disillusionment. One of them, Pablo, comes to the conclusion that he was murdered because, in his depressive state, "he began to feel certain that he was possessed. Not as if by magic but by his own gift. His own voracious hunger for sound became like a demon. Another body within him that lashed out without warning. That took hold of him and swept him away. . . . He was desperate for some kind of help so he turned to religion. Superstition. Cultism. There were plenty of self-proclaimed 'healers' ready to take him on . . . his music turned into boring melodies. . . . Finally he decided to leave them completely. And that's when they killed him."[38] Though Pablo does not get the particulars of the story correct, his assertion that Niles felt threatened by his own talent is accurate, and it reminds readers of both Hoss and Cody, who were, essentially, trapped by their talents into meaningless roles. More important, the constant references to anxiety about controlling one's talent suggest that Shepard is commenting on his own insecurities as an artist.

Like Shepard, Niles engages in an "experimental" kind of art that breaks conventions and reimagines traditions. Niles's art could be described as similar in motivation to Shepard's. Though Niles is a musician, his experimental band plays visual music: onstage the actors interact with various instruments, but absolutely no sound is made. The pitch is supposedly too high for humans to comprehend. More than one critic has described Shepard's work as a kind of translation of music into a visual aesthetic. In the world of the artist, Pablo becomes the critic. He attacks experimentation as art for art's sake and maintains that such art is interested only in destruction. He claims it only relates "to breaking with tradition! To breaking off with the past! To throwing the diligent efforts of our forefathers and their forefathers before them to the winds! To turning the classics to garbage before our very eyes! To distorting the very foundations of our cherished values! To making mincemeat out of brilliance! . . . To changing the shape of American morality! That's where it's at! That's where it's at, isn't it! You've snuck up on us through the back door."[39] Pablo's criticism recalls the early reaction of critics to Shepard's inscrutable one-acts. Without the context of the play, Pablo's words could easily read as the conventional theatrical world's view of Shepard: he is "not strong enough to take us over by direct political action," and chooses instead "to drive us all crazy."

But if there were any question that Niles becomes Shepard's new stand-in as the tortured artist, the protagonist's confession to Paullette about his past makes the autobiographical implications of the play clear. Reminiscing about his childhood, he relates a memory of living on an island with his mother that comes directly from Shepard's own past. He tells her of living "in a house with a corrugated roof that sounded like Balinese cymbals when it rained. . . . And mom has the .45 sitting right there loaded on her lap in case any gooks stick their heads in the window. She'd blow their heads right off."[40] Shepard establishes Niles as his proxy, and then has the character deconstruct his artistic slump by concluding that the artist's problem lies in his inability to be original anymore. In a statement that could be made by

Hoss, Cody, or Shepard himself, Niles confesses, "I'm repeating myself, again and again. It's not even myself I'm repeating. I'm repeating them. Over and over. They talk to me all the time. THERE'S VOICES COMING AT ME!"[41]

Paullette's cure for Niles's quickly deteriorating art is to destroy the parts of his personality that won't leave him alone. In a nod to Shepard's earliest play, *Cowboys,* Paullette starts the symbolic murder spree with the figure of the cowboy. Niles refuses to slaughter him, however:

NILES: Why does he have to go?

PAULLETTE: He's burning your time.

NILES: He's a hero, Paullette. He discovered a whole way of life. He ate
    rattlesnakes for breakfast. Chicago wouldn't even exist if it wasn't for
    him. He drove cattle right into Chicago's front door. Towns sprang up
    wherever he stopped to wet his whistle. Crime flourished all around
    him. The law was a joke to him. State lines. He sang songs to the
    Milky Way. . . . You can't kill a hero!

PAULLETTE: He's no hero! He's a weasel! He's a punk psychopath built
    into a big deal by crummy New England rags.

NILES: He's a myth!

PAULLETTE: So are you!

NILES: You can't kill a myth![42]

The mock murder does not work. Instead of destroying the mythic figure of the cowboy, Paullette's arrows fly into one of the detectives onstage. The symbolic narrative seeps over onto the literal narrative, and the connections between Shepard's and Niles's art are highlighted through the interplay of the competing tales attempting to destroy Niles's personas, Paullette instead destroys one of Shepard's. The play breaks down into a Pirandellian tale where characters begin to acknowledge their artificiality and reference their performance in the spectacle taking place in front of the audience.

Paullette, too, can be seen as a part of the personality of Niles/Shepard. Obsessed with authenticity and singularity, she reminds both Niles and Shepard that their art should define their persona, not the other way around. To her the cowboy is not symbolic and meaningful: he is instead a ruse, a guise. Like the plays that come immediately before it, *Suicide in B-flat* moves from being a riff on the mystery of one man to a meditation on maintaining the role of artist in a public world. It clearly expresses Shepard's own anxieties over the responsibilities of being an artist, and as one critic noted, it explores the difficult transition from public persona to artist. No longer a public spectacle, Shepard had to deal with the weight of being "most-promising-young-award-winning-soon-to-be-a-major-talented-playwright-as-commodity."[43]

However, while Shepard remained unsure of how he would reshape his art and make himself relevant again, he already had begun the process of redefining himself. Unlike before, his ideas did not come from the realm of the experimental theatrical world, with its emphases on language play, fragments, and mythic worlds. Instead his subject came to be the mundane world of the American family and its hidden secrets. By working through his early obsessions with rock 'n' roll, language, heroes, and revolution, Shepard created a vivid world and compelling cast of characters that eventually morphed into a more naturalistic aesthetic. From the exploration of his new muse—the American family—Shepard created three plays that came to define his career. The first piece of his family trilogy, *Curse of the Starving Class* (1977), moved away from the outlandish settings of plays such as *Operation Sidewinder* and *Forensic and the Navigators* and, instead, took place in the most traditional and ordinary setting for an American play: the family kitchen.

CHAPTER 3

Divining the Cure
Curse of the Starving Class

Curse of the Starving Class represents a fundamental break from the aesthetic of Shepard's early plays for a number of reasons. First, and foremost, the play comprises nine characters, not two or three. And all the characters have semirealistic relationships with one another within the family. Instead of having long monologues bookended by absurd, chaotic action, the play follows a linear plot that gradually builds to a climax. And, finally, the play employs the familiar three-act structure of other American dramas that explore families. If Shepard's early work signaled that he would be a dramatist who would experiment with language, form, and character, *Curse of the Starving Class* manifests a playwright with the ability to use those unique ideas in familiar structures. While the play uses familiar elements of realistic drama—techniques Shepard had not experimented much with before—it does not establish a brand new trajectory for Shepard and his art. Rather the play takes the themes and preoccupations Shepard explored in his early pieces (such as power struggles, violence, and the mystery of identity) and expands them into a full-length exploration of a single family's complicated relationships.

The tradition of the American family drama had been established long before *Curse of the Starving Class,* and Shepard's movement into that familiar territory suddenly set him apart from the avant-garde storyteller of plays such as *Operation Sidewinder.* He became an American dramatist in the mold of Arthur Miller, Eugene O'Neill, and Tennessee Williams. Aside from dealing with a conventional topic, Shepard's aesthetic in *Curse of the Starving Class* drew from the "kitchen sink realism" that he had spent much of his early years inverting. While the set of the play is sparse, the characters do interact with realistic props of familiar domestic life: a refrigerator, a stove, and a breakfast table. And even though the rhythms of his characters' speech are musical and indicative of instruments in an orchestra, there is no rock 'n' roll music, no five-page long soliloquies that undercut the action of the play. Coming to *Curse of the Starving Class* without any knowledge of Shepard's early plays, one might reasonably conceive of the author as a traditional realist.

The play revolves around a small California family. The father, Weston, suffers fits of drunken rage that have gradually undermined the stability of the familial relationships. At the beginning we learn that, enraged by a night of drunken carousing, he has tried to enter the house by kicking in a locked door. The play opens with Wesley, his son, attempting to repair the damage to the door. Meanwhile Ella, the mother, and Emma, her daughter, spar verbally over topics from menstruation to money, and Ella reveals she plans to sell the house and property to a lawyer, Taylor, without Weston's knowledge. When a drunk Weston appears after sleeping off his night of debauchery, he reveals to Wesley that he has also sold the house and property to a local bar owner, Ellis, for fifteen hundred dollars, precisely the amount he owes to cover some gambling debts.

Quickly the family and house itself begin to unravel, as Wesley confronts both Taylor and Ellis about his father's debts. When Ellis learns that Emma has ridden through his bar destroying it with shots from a rifle, he angrily takes back the money he had promised Weston. Wesley attempts to get the money back but is instead roughed up by Ellis. He returns, defeated, to confront his father, who, newly sober, has both fixed the door he demolished and decided not to sell the land and house after all. Wesley tells his father that he should leave the house because the loan sharks he owes money to will certainly find him there; despite his feeling that he has begun a new existence, Weston does escape to Mexico to protect himself. Emma comes home from jail only to embark on a life of crime. After wishing Wesley good-bye, she gets in the car to head off, but the loan sharks arrive and detonate the automobile (with Emma still inside). The two men come into the house to threaten Wesley, who, in his father's clothes, they initially mistake for Weston. After they leave, mother and son sit alone and contemplate the legacy of Weston and his impact on their lives.

Shepard initially declared that the subject of the American family was not compelling enough to sustain an entire play, but in *Curse of the Starving Class*, he signaled his investment in the formation, structure, and dynamics of families in general. The play seems concerned with the "tortured question[s] of why the family is a family at all, with what a family actually *is* and how it holds together (if indeed it does) in a world stripped of old consequences and certainties."[1] Throughout *Curse of the Starving Class,* characters interrogate their own identities, as "father" or "son," or members of a "class" or "society," only to find no connection between those roles (familial and/ or social) and their perceptions of themselves. The end result is that the family exists almost by accident. It becomes a tenuous connection, no more meaningful than strangers who share the same space. Wesley emphasizes the lack of connection among the family when he responds to Emma's offhand remark that he had done the best he could in trying to get Weston's money back: "I didn't do a thing. . . . I just grew up here."[2]

The children's engagement with their evolving masculinity and femininity complicates not only the notion of family identity but also sexual and gender identity. Wesley is caught up in the mystery of becoming a man—and Emma a woman—without understanding the consequences of such a transformation. Eventually each character in the family struggles with the consequences of their gendered identity that, much like their familial identity, is predetermined, seemingly accidental, and, ultimately, inescapable. In this sense *Curse of the Starving Class* moves from the simple exploration of an American family and into the familiar territory of Shepard's earlier plays, including the revising of gender roles and the purposeful deconstruction of identity in relation to social and familial discourses.

The play's title refers to the family's multiple frustrations with identity, and it underscores a continual and almost bestial hunger (both physical and figurative). While each character does different business onstage, they all repeat the action of opening the refrigerator to look for something to eat. Food is referenced throughout the play: characters eat onstage (Ella eats bacon, eggs, and toast; Weston enjoys a two-helping breakfast of ham and eggs; and Wesley throws the contents of the refrigerator onto the floor and devours them like an animal), and artichokes boil furiously for much of act 2. Similarly Emma is involved in a 4-H demonstration on how to cut up a chicken to fry, while Wesley raises, feeds, and cares for lambs, which will later be butchered for food. It is also significant that the land the family lives on was once used to grow avocados, a pursuit that Weston encourages Wesley to continue in act 3.

Shepard's emphasis on the trope of food also references a figurative hunger, the dissatisfaction of the family members with their identity, both within the family and their social sphere; Ella and Weston are caught in the paralyzing inability to obtain the "American dream" of self-authored social mobility: they consistently remain hungry and unsatisfied, wanting more even when their refrigerator is full. Though the parents of the family strongly argue that they are not a poor, lower-class family that cannot afford to feed their children, Shepard shows the truth of the situation. Both Weston and Ella fail in their individual attempts to renegotiate their social status by selling a property that belongs to the entire family. All these attempts to deny, redefine, and "rise" above their lack of money lead to disaster, including the home's eventual sale to land-grabbing developers and the death of Emma at the hands of the loan sharks to whom Weston owes money.

Production History

Many actors whose names are now familiar to contemporary audiences—John Malkovich, Gary Sinise, Bradley Whitford, Olympia Dukakis, and Kathy Bates—got their first exposure in performances of *Curse of the Starving Class*. Because of its sparse set and small cast, it has been one of Shepard's most easily produced plays. *Curse of the Starving Class* first premiered at the Royal Court in London in April 1977 and made its American premiere in New York City at Joseph Papp's Public Theater in March 1978. Of its London opening, one critic declared that the play is "an old-fashioned, evidently autobiographical, family problem play" that "works better and more creatively on the symbolic level."[3] Harold Clurman of the *Nation* celebrated the play's American premiere as both "ungainly and wonderful," adding, "Its faults are part of its virtues. Shepard improvises on a theme; at times he seems to leap or meander away from it . . . there is imagination and a particular sort of poetry throughout."[4] Clurman found James Gammon's Weston "rugged, comic and pathetic," while Olympia Dukakis's Ella "creates a reality that borders on fantasy."[5] While the reviews for the New York opening were positive, the play ran for only five weeks.

Though it was produced multiple times between 1978 and 1985, perhaps the most ambitious revival of the play started at the famous off-Broadway venue the Promenade Theater in 1985 and ran for 295 performances through the next year when it moved to Theatre 890. That cast included Karen Tull, Eddie Jones, and Bradley Whitford, and, in what was clearly becoming a vehicle for strong actresses, the character of Ella was portrayed by a young Kathy Bates. Critic Rush Rehm noted that, while the performances were strong throughout, the director's attempt at staging the play as a "classical" text did not work: the action of the play felt mythic and stilted despite the work being only being seven years old.[6] What works for the play, Rehm noted, was Shepard's unique comic style "drawn from physical comedy, the language of poetic drama, surrealism, modern jazz, the symbolism of Christianity, the Hollywood gangster film, as well as . . . the absurdists."[7]

The performance drew Shepard and his newly pregnant partner Jessica Lange; after sitting through the performance in the back row, Shepard "went backstage . . . and told the cast they'd done a good job."[8]

The revival also led to an embarrassing cable television remake in 1994. The overwrought teleplay (written by Bruce Beresford, who directed Shepard in the comedy *Crimes of the Heart* in 1986) exploded the nuances of Shepard's script into overdrawn caricature. Although the play had been a serious meditation on family, the movie became "overemphatic and sentimental. Except for Kathy Bates, reprising her performance as the mother in the successful off-Broadway revival, the roles are badly cast and badly acted."[9] Instead of gaining traction for Shepard and his play, the television movie represented its source material badly. Since that debacle the play has been produced multiple times through the 1990s and 2000s. Notable productions include Chicago's Steppenwolf Theatre's 1991 production and Yale Repertory Theater's revival of the play in 2000, the latter of which critics felt upheld Shepard's initial vision "of the spiritual starvation of America and the American family imprisoned in smithereens on a farm"[10] Despite being written more than thirty-five years ago, *Curse of the Starving Class* still compels its audience to meditate on the problems of family and on the complexities of identity, topics that remain relevant in contemporary America.

Professional and Personal Influence

To an audience familiar with Sam Shepard's life, *Curse of the Starving Class* clearly engages with portions of Shepard's adolescence and his relationship with his father. Stephen Bottoms suggested that Shepard's play came from a conscious desire to piece together his own identity from the earliest memories he had as a boy. His goal was to "confront and embrace his origins, rather than avoid them."[11] Much of the exploration of his identity led him back to his father. Shepard biographer Don Shewey noted that the significance of *Curse*'s exploration of the family can be tied to the playwright's own blossoming experiences with his father: in 1976 Shepard began receiving what Shewey referred to as "Hi, Steve" letters from his father—a correspondence that centered on requests for money and emotional confessions.[12] The new contact with his father brought up old demons for Shepard, and his thoughts turned to the ways in which family can affect identity forever: "Certain things that occur inside the family often leave marks on the emotional life and are far stronger than fantasy. What might be seen as the fantasy is, to me, just a kind of rumination on those deep marks, a manifestation of the emotional and psychological elements. The thing is not to avoid the issue but to see that it exists."[13] *Curse of the Starving Class* became, for Shepard, a way of acknowledging the deep emotional marks left behind by his family life and an honest attempt to piece together how those wounds affected his identity.

The play also comes from anxiety over his identity. Before beginning the play, Shepard made a huge decision to move from London; he did not move back to New York and the familiar theater scene he had left behind, but rather to California, the land of his boyhood and adolescence. It was a move that, according to Shewey, was rooted in family. In California the focus of Shepard's writing switched from "drugs, jazz, theater, and rock 'n' roll" and to more deliberate "thoughts of home and . . . the direction of family."[14] In 1970 the birth of Shepard's first son, Jesse Mojo Shepard, changed his life. Now Shepard was not just a partner, but a father himself. Thoughts of his boyhood shifted into thoughts on the role of the father in a son's life. From the newly formed relationship with his father to Shepard's own experiences "building a family of his own and thinking about the one that produced him,"[15] *Curse of the Starving Class* became part of a new obsession with the idea of family itself: How does it form? How does it exist? And how does it define—largely beyond our control or desire—who we are and how we are perceived?

As Shepard's first "traditional" play, *Curse of the Starving Class* also clearly owes a debt to the dramatists who came before Shepard and to their work with the subject of family. Shepard set the play in the middle of an avocado orchard, with expanses of trees and fields across the property, and in some ways, *Curse of the Starving Class* can be seen as a reimagining of Chekhov's *The Cherry Orchard*. The plots of both plays share surface similarities, including families in crisis and their attempts to sell their property in hopes of escaping an inevitable decline. Throughout Shepard's play Wesley and Weston reference their dwindling "orchard" and their hope to see it produce fruit again. While one early reviewer of the play called it "*The Cherry Orchard* returning as farce,"[16] Stephen Bottoms has said of the connections between Chekhov and Shepard, "The family's home is invaded by a collection of marvelously plastic property speculators and gangsters, bidding to turn their avocado orchard into low-rent housing . . . as part of the inexorable march of progress."[17] Critic Charles Lyons has found a similar connection between Shepard's presentation of the father and the framework of Chekhov's larger works: "Shepard's problematizing of the father figure is conventional. In all of Chekhov's major works, the father's absence contributes to the deteriorating state of the immediate environment."[18] While such a "unashamedly derivative" plot borrowed partly from one of the masters of realist drama might invite criticism, Bottoms argued that Shepard's connection should be read not as pastiche but as "emphasis" as it plays on the form and structure of a familiar idea; Shepard's allusion to Chekhov is, after all, "deliberate, a formal device."[19]

In much the same way Shepard's plot references Chekhov's, he also alludes to themes, characters, and structures familiar to American drama throughout *Curse of the Starving Class*. Bottoms has noted the connection between the play and O'Neill's *Desire under the Elms*, both of which explore "darkly destructive family traits repeating themselves down the generations,"[20] a theme that Bottoms follows all the way back to Greek tragedy. To be sure, Shepard references the tragedy of the sins of the father being visited upon the children throughout *Curse of the Starving Class*, and O'Neill's presence as father of the American family drama is keenly felt by American audiences familiar with his works.

However, some of the allusions to Shepard's American dramatic mentors might be less obvious. The allusions to Tennessee Williams's plays, for example, are made primarily through humorous dialogue that slyly references the author's memorable quotations. When Weston decides to change his life, the monologue he addresses to Wesley reminds the audience of Big Daddy's resolve at the end of *Cat on a Hot Tin Roof* to look over his property early in the morning and see what belongs to him: "It's real peaceful up here. Especially at that time a' the morning. Then it struck me that I actually was the owner. That somehow it was me and I was actually the one walking on my own piece of land. And that gave me a great feeling."[21] And when Wesley interrogates his mother about the financial arrangements on the house, Ella yells him down with "I HAVE A LAWYER FRIEND!," mimicking the famous scene between Stella and Stanley Kowalski in *A Streetcar Named Desire*.

While Shepard mines familiar ground, borrowing idea, plots, characters, and even language from many of the titans of realist drama, he does so with action that is largely symbolic and with devices that more often would be found in expressionist drama. The play may take place in a realistic setting with actual set pieces that offer clues as to the layout of the house, but the exploration of identity subverts whatever realism Shepard offers the audience in the opening scene. While Shepard borrows heavily from the superficial details of realist drama, his true goals are more concerned with deconstructing the figurative landscape of the American family. His intent is to expose the metaphorical and symbolic order of the family, revise the notion of gendered and social identities, and explore the potential for escape from the emotional inheritance of our parents.

Shifting Identities: Female Troubles

If there is one theme that recurs throughout *Curse of the Starving Class* it is a palpable confusion over the shifting nature of identities, especially gendered, familial, and social. At the very beginning of the play, we are confronted with a "birds and bees" lecture given to Emma about her transition into womanhood. Though Ella wants to present her daughter with "all the facts" about her period before she hears "a lot of lies" from her friends about it, Ella herself is clearly confused about the process of menstruation: she cautions, "Now, the first thing is you should never go swimming when that happens. It can cause you to bleed to death. The water draws it out of you" (139). Passing on to her daughter a mythic and absolutely false idea of the "dangers" of menstruation, Ella signals that she, too, was mis-informed about the particulars of her transformation from girlhood to womanhood by her mother. Ella cannot even communicate the basic facts about the menstruation cycle to Emma. When she tries to tell Emma about the sterilization of "sanitary napkins," the conversation gets bogged down in the idiosyncrasies of language:

EMMA: How come they call them napkins?
ELLA: Well, I don't know. I didn't make it up. Somebody called them
    napkins a long time ago and it just stuck.
EMMA: "Sanitary napkins."
ELLA: Yes.
EMMA: It's a funny sound. Like a hospital or something.
ELLA: Well, that's what they should be like, but unfortunately they're not.
    They're not hospital clean that's for sure. And you should know that
    anything you stick up in there should be absolutely hospital clean.
EMMA: Stick up in where? (139–40)

Here Shepard's humor hides a dark truth: a crucial mother-daughter dialogue about the changes inherent in puberty ends with Emma still having no idea about either the meaning of menstruation or how to handle it.

The cycle of misinformation is one of the many "curses" handed down from father to son and mother to daughter, but, in this context, Shepard clearly references Eve's "curse" of menstruation. Later in the act, Emma asks why she is too young to leave the house but not too young "to have babies": "that's what bleeding is, right? That's what bleeding's for" (147–48). Instead of answering her question, Ella simply counters, "Don't talk silly, and go change your uniform." Unable to connect her new reality to her mother's femininity, Emma remains unsure of the meaning and responsibilities of becoming a woman. When she finally gets to speak to an outsider, Taylor, her mother's lawyer, she grills him for answers about the mystery of femininity, asking him whether her mother also menstruates: "Does she bleed? . . . You know. Does she have blood coming out of her" (152). Taylor, however, also refuses to answer her questions. As Ella leaves, she asks Wesley, "Keep an eye out for Emma, Wes. She's got the curse. You know what that's like for a girl, the first time around" (155). The irony is not lost on the audience: as a teenage boy, Wesley has no idea "what that's like for a girl," and, sadly, neither does Emma.

With the freedom afforded her by her ignorance of the responsibilities and meaning of being a woman, Emma dreams of running away from her family, going to Mexico and working hard, masculine jobs: "I was going to work on fishing boats. Deep sea fishing. Helping businessmen haul in huge swordfish and barracuda. I was going to work my away along the coast, stopping at all the little towns, speaking Spanish. I was going to learn be a mechanic and work on four-wheel-drive vehicles that broke down. Transmissions. I could've learned to fix anything. Then I'd be a short-order cook and write novels on the side. In the kitchen. Kitchen novels. Then I'd get published and disappear into Mexico. Just like that guy . . . who wrote *Treasure of the Sierra Madre*" (149). She is brought back from her reverie by a runaway horse and her mother's denial that such a dream is possible for a woman: "Snap out of it, Emma. You don't have that kind of a background to do jobs like that. That's not for you, that stuff. You can do beautiful embroidery; why do you want to be a mechanic?" (149).

Later, with Wesley, Emma imagines the same dream as the ultimate revenge against her mother and her new "boyfriend," Taylor. She imagines another fantasy, but this time she creates a story about how her mother and Taylor escape the family by crossing the border and living at campsites across the beaches of Mexico. Inevitably their car dies near a town where she is the only mechanic: "They don't recognize me, though. They ask if I can fix their 'carro,' and I speak only Spanish. I've lost the knack for English by now." In her fantasy she fixes the car overnight by removing Ella and Taylor's perfectly serviceable engine and replacing it with a "rebuilt Volkswagen block. In the morning, I charge them double for labor, see them on their way, and then resell their engine for a small mint" (161–62). The revenge fantasy involves Emma shifting from her familial identity as the subjugated sister and daughter into a competent, powerful, and masculine role. Wesley this time interrupts Emma's reverie to ask her to attend to her feminine domestic duties of cooking:

WESLEY: If you're not doing anything, would you check the artichokes?
EMMA: I am doing something.
WESLEY: What
EMMA: I'm remaking my charts.
WESLEY: What do you spend your time on that stuff for? You should be
   doing more important stuff.
EMMA: Like checking artichokes?
WESLEY: Yeah!
EMMA: You check the artichokes. I'm busy.
WESLEY: You're on the rag. (162)

The exchange between brother and sister highlights a frustration over the singularity of the woman's role within the family. Within the typical structure of the American family, Shepard argues that the role of women is strictly defined by domestic duties. A drunk Weston emphasizes the traditional role of women in a family when he shows up with his laundry; he expects only Ella, the mother, to do it. When Emma offers, Weston bites back: "No, you won't do it! You let her do it! It's her job! What does she do around here anyway? Do you know? What does she do all day long? What does a woman do?" The question, posed to Emma, who has just begun her transition from girlhood to womanhood, is a poignant one, not unlike her answer: "I don't know" (166).

Indeed much of what women do is guessed at throughout the play. The mystery of femininity is a discourse that is to be saved for only Ella and Emma, to be pieced together from largely mythic sources. When Wesley tells his father that Emma has had her first period, the man is shocked that the boy even knows such information: "What happens when I'm gone, you all sit around and talk about your periods? You're not supposed to know when your sister has her period! That's confidential between women. They keep it a secret that means" (167). For Weston and Wesley, femininity represents a dark secret that is shared only between women and should not be spoken by men. However, Emma and Ella rarely talk about femininity, and when they do, their speech is coded, misinformed, and false.

When Ella returns from her date with Taylor, Wesley confronts her with the news that Weston has already sold the property to a local businessman. He chastises her for trying to redefine her role within the family as the head of the house and cautions that his father is "going to kill" her for it. After a brief pause, Ella remarks on the curse of her place in the family in strongly feminine terms: "Do you know what this is? It's a curse. I can feel it. It's invisible but it's there. It's always there. It comes onto us like nighttime.

Every day I can feel it. Every day I can see it coming. And it always comes. Repeats itself. It comes even when you do everything to stop it from coming. Even when you try and change it. And it goes back. Deep. It goes back and back to tiny little cells and genes. To atoms. To tiny little swimming things making up their minds without us. Plotting in the womb. Before that even. In the air. We're surrounded with it. It's bigger than the government even. It goes forward too. We spread it. We pass it on. We inherit it and pass it down, and then pass it down again. It goes on and on like that without us" (173–74). Like menstruation, the curse she references is cyclical: it comes and goes, repeating. And it has an insidious control over her life. And the curse represents a power that is beyond any control, predetermined and inescapable. Ella may be commenting on the curse of family (especially in her reference to genes), but more than likely her speech references the curse of gender identity and its powerful hold on the lives of the family members.

At the end of act 2, we learn that Emma has tried to fulfill her masculine fantasy by becoming a cowboy anarchist. She rides through Ellis's bar with her father's rifle and shoots "the place full of holes" (179). Transgressing beyond feminine boundaries, Emma is locked up and thrown in juvenile detention until her parents can buy her bond. When Ella confronts Weston with the news of their daughter's arrest, he takes pride in her criminal trespasses not because they invert her place in the family but, in fact, because they affirm her connection to the bloodline:

WESTON: What'd they nab her for?

ELLA: Possession of firearms. Malicious vandalism. Breaking and entering. Assault. Violation of equestrian regulations. You name it.

WESTON: Well, she always was a fireball.

ELLA: Part of the inheritance, right?

WESTON: Right. Direct descendant.

ELLA: Well, I'm glad you've found a way of turning shame into a source of pride.

WESTON: What's shameful about it? Takes courage to get charged with all that stuff. It's not everyone her age who can run up a list of credits like that.

ELLA: That's for sure.

WESTON: Could you?

ELLA: Don't be ridiculous! I'm not self-destructive. Doesn't run in my family line.

WESTON: That's right. I never thought about it like that. You're the only one who doesn't have it. Only us. (188)

Despite Emma's attempts to escape the family and her inherited role as subjugated daughter and sister, she cannot escape her connection to femininity. When she appears for the last time in act 3, she confesses to Wesley that she escaped juvenile detention only by using her feminine wiles: "I made sexual overtures to the sergeant. . . . Easy" (196). Doomed to an identity crafted for her by her mother, Emma decides to escape one final time into a life of crime, her revenge for her mother's suffocating perspective on femininity. Her escape is thwarted a final time when loan sharks after her father explode the car she was using to run away.

The Mystery of Masculinity

In the same way Ella misinforms Emma about what it means to be a woman, Weston confuses Wesley about the responsibilities of masculinity through his poor lessons. Early in the play Ella conflates Weston and Wesley's masculinity with the potential for explosive violence. Threatening Taylor, who has come to visit her mother when Weston is not at home, she notes that her father had "almost killed one guy he caught her with":

EMMA: A short fuse they call it. Runs in the family. His father was just like him. And his father before him. And his father before him. Wesley is just like Pop, too. Like liquid dynamite.
TAYLOR: Liquid dynamite?
EMMA: Yeah. What's that stuff called?
TAYLOR: I don't know.
EMMA: It's chemical. It's the same thing that makes him drink. Something in the blood. Hereditary. Highly explosive.
TAYLOR: Sounds dangerous.
EMMA: Yeah.
TAYLOR: Don't you get afraid living in an environment like this?
EMMA: No. The fear lies with the ones who carry the stuff in their blood, not the ones who don't. I don't have it in me. (152)

Recognizing that, as Weston's daughter, she lacks the same "liquid dynamite . . . in the blood" that infects Wesley, Emma connects the family's conception of masculinity with a potentially destructive violence. That threat is clear from Weston's initial destruction of the door (an offstage moment that occurs before the play begins) as well as Wesley's pathological need to fight for his father's money at the end of the play. Like Emma, Wesley dreams of moving far away from the family's home to Alaska, "the frontier . . . full of possibilities" (163), but he recognizes that, as the only son, his responsibility is to make sure that he protects his home. Instead of attempting to escape like

Emma, he settles himself in the house, trying to fashion a door and protect the land like the responsible head of the family.

Wesley tries to understand the secret of masculinity, but he cannot piece it together from the clues offered by his parents. Early in the play Ella remarks that Wesley has the potential to be "sensitive" like her father was, but that he has turned mean, like his own father. But her perspective on masculinity connects a man's emotional life to purely physical characteristics: "I always thought you were just like him, but you're not, are you? . . . Why aren't you? You're circumcized [sic] just like him. It's almost identical in fact" (143–44). While Ella wishes Wesley would be more like her father, the boy is instead growing up to be the spitting image of Weston, despite the efforts by the boy to escape his fate. Though Weston belittles Wesley and calls him stupid, the old man instills in Wesley his viewpoint:

WESTON: Look at my outlook. You don't envy it, right?

WESLEY: No.

WESTON: That's because it's full of poison. Infected. And you recognize poison, right? You recognize it when you see it?

WESLEY: Yes.

WESTON: Yes, you do. I can see that you do. My poison scares you.

WESLEY: Doesn't scare me.

WESTON: No?

WESLEY: No.

WESTON: Good. You're growing up. I never saw my old man's poison until I was much older than you. Much older. And then you know how I recognized it? . . . Because I saw myself infected with it. That's how. I saw me carrying it around. His poison in my body. You think that's fair? (167)

Shepard's use of phallic imagery here (especially the connection to "seeing" the poison) reminds the audience of the disconnect between the emotional lives of fathers and sons and their physical characteristics. Masculinity becomes a "disease" that "infects" father and son throughout the play. Like Emma, Wesley cannot fathom the mystery of his masculinity; he imagines it as something concrete, approachable.

Wesley's attempts to "learn" masculinity from his father all end in frustration. Wesley cannot understand what it means to be a man just by watching. Weston, on the other hand, learned his role from surreptitiously observing his father: "You know I watched my old man move around. I watched him move through rooms. I watched him drive tractors, watched him watching baseball, watched him keeping out of the way of things. Out of the way of my mother. Away from my brothers. Watched him on the sidelines. Nobody saw him but me. Everybody was right here, but nobody saw him but me. He lived apart. Right in the midst of things and he lived apart. Nobody saw that" (168). Weston's understanding of masculinity from his father comes in the form of disconnection, separation. Like his father, Weston attempts to separate himself from the other members of the family but cautions Wesley against attempting to learn masculinity from him. It is a secret he will hold inside for the entirety of his life: "You can watch me all you want to," he tells the boy. "You won't find out a thing" (169).

In act 3 Weston attempts to start over, to redefine himself. He reasserts his role as the man of the house by fixing the door he had smashed, thus protecting his family and home from intruders. He removes his "old clothes" and walks through the house "in my birthday suit": "it was like peeling off a whole person. A whole stranger" (185). He takes a hot bath and does the family's laundry in a reversal of his masculine role. The end result is that Weston feels as though he has changed. Though the only significant difference is his clean body and clothes, he feels that he has fundamentally changed his identity. He decides he will no longer be the drunk and irresponsible father to a dysfunctional family but will instead save the farm, the family, and his honor. His plan, however, fails, as Wesley reminds him of the debt he owes to the loan sharks: "Maybe you've changed, but you still owe them" (192). Despite his new lease on life, Weston cannot escape his past, and he realizes, with regret, that while he was drinking and gambling, searching for an escape, what he really wanted was his family: "I kept looking for it out there somewhere. And all the time it was right inside the house" (194). Unable to remain on the land he owns, he flees to Mexico in order to outrun his demons.

With his father gone, Wesley attempts to become the man of the house, but his decision is as whimsical as his father's desire to change and just as superficial: he puts on his father's old clothes. Emma notes the ridiculousness of his sudden change as she returns from prison: "You're sick! What're you doing with his clothes on? Are you supposed to be the head of the family now or something? The Big Cheese? Daddy Bear?" (195). Wesley believes that by putting on the clothes of his father, he can somehow fathom the mystery of his masculine identity. And, for a few minutes, it works: "I started putting all his clothes on. His baseball cap, his tennis shoes, his overcoat. And every time I put one thing on it seemed like a part of him was growing on me. I could feel him taking over me. . . . I could feel myself retreating. I could feel him coming in and me going out. Just like the change of the guards" (196). But in the end the change of clothes does not change Wesley's identity. When

Emerson and Slater come to rough up Weston, they initially are confused (as is Ella) by Wesley's costume, but they quickly come to understand he is just a boy: "Oh, and if you see your old man, you might pass on the info. We hate to keep repeating ourselves" (199). Weston's masculinity remains a secret from Wesley, who, in his father's absence, can only play at what it means to be a man.

If Weston wishes to keep his masculinity a secret, he offers some clues about his perspective through a story that he repeats to the family about castrating spring lambs. Remembering back to a time when he was "out in the fields" long ago, Weston reminisces about how, as he emasculated each lamb, a tremendous eagle would swoop down from the sky almost as though it were taunting him. Finally Weston realizes what the bird wanted: "He was after those testes. Those fresh little remnants of manlihood" (183). Weston toys with the bird by throwing the severed testes on the roof, and as the eagle crashes down to retrieve them, he finds himself strangely moved by the entire scene: "Somethin' brought me straight up off the ground and I started yellin' my head off. I don't know why it was comin' outa' me but I was standing there with this icy feeling up my backbone and just . . . cheerin' for that eagle" (183).

As a parable about masculinity, Weston's story suggests the indescribable "feeling" he gets watching the eagle attack and devour the site of masculinity in the lamb's genitals is, in essence, a celebration of his own masculine identity. Significantly, as Weston recounts his story to the sick lamb in the kitchen, he is interrupted by Wesley, who asks to hear the rest of the story. True to his word, his father refuses to offer his son a glimpse into his perspective on the masculine world: "I ain't telling it again!" (184). However, it is Wesley and Ella who end the anecdote for the audience at the closing of the play by transforming it from a celebration of masculinity to a vicious fight between the eagle and a tomcat:

ELLA: That's right. A big tom cat comes. Right out in the fields. And he jumps up on top of that roof to sniff around in all the entrails or whatever it was.
WESLEY: And that eagle comes down and picks up the cat in his talons and carries him screaming off into the sky.
ELLA: That's right. And they fight. They fight like crazy in the middle of the sky. . . . And they come crashing down to earth. Both of them come crashing down. Like one whole thing. (200)

The movement from parable celebrating masculinity to a story about the potential devastation left by competing masculinities signifies the tragedy of

Shepard's play. Besides referencing Emerson and Slater, the men who have just blown up Weston's car (with his daughter still inside), Wesley and Ella's final ending to Weston's story suggests that the mystery of masculinity always deepens into a violent confrontation. Critic Bert Cardullo has reminded us, too, that, just as in the eagle and cat story, every character in *Curse of the Starving Class* remains damaged at the end: "Weston goes off to Mexico to escape his creditors, while Ella is abandoned by Taylor and left with nothing."[22] And Wesley ends the play with no clearer idea of what it means to be a man other than fighting for your family's honor and fixing the door of the family home. The audience leaves him still a boy, only in the clothing of a man, a curious paradox that Shepard addresses in the two other plays in his family trilogy.

The Starving Class: Social Identities

Shepard's repetition of the phrase "starving class" throughout the play highlights another of his chief thematic concerns: an inescapable and inevitable class identity that afflicts this family despite their insistence otherwise. It is clear early in the play that the family Shepard explores does not belong to the middle class. When Emma wants to swim at a neighbor's house, she describes the pool longingly: "The Thompsons have a new heated pool. You should see it, Ma. They even got blue lights around it at night. It's really beautiful. Like a fancy hotel" (139). But perhaps the biggest clue Shepard gives to the family's class identity is through the set piece of the refrigerator, which every family member addresses at one point or another during the play.

When Emma learns that her mother has taken the chicken she raised from infancy and boiled it for dinner, she explodes into a fit of rage. Though Ella claims that she ate the chicken because she was "starving," Emma shouts from offstage:

EMMA'S VOICE: NO ONE'S STARVING IN THIS HOUSE! YOU'RE FEEDING
   YOUR FACE RIGHT NOW!
ELLA: So what!
EMMA'S VOICE: SO NO ONE'S STARVING! WE DON'T BELONG TO THE
   STARVING CLASS!
ELLA: Don't speak unless you know what you're speaking about! There's
   no such thing as a starving class!
EMMA'S VOICE: THERE IS SO! THERE'S A STARVING CLASS OF PEOPLE, AND
   WE'RE NOT PART OF IT!
ELLA: WE'RE HUNGRY, AND THAT'S STARVING ENOUGH FOR ME! (142)

The family understands itself in a continuum of class hierarchies but defines itself in opposition to the bottom rung, disconnected from poverty, or, as Ella tells Wesley, "We're not poor. We're not rich but we're not poor" (143).

The action of the play stems largely from Ella and Weston's inability to handle the finances of the house. While Ella decides to sell the property to Taylor, a con man who has already swindled her husband out of money, Weston cannot pay his gambling debts and decides to cover them by selling the property to Ellis, the owner of his favorite bar. Both have dreams of getting rich. Ella tells Wesley she has a plan to turn the family around: "We're going to have some money real soon. . . . I'll let you know when the time comes." In her fantasy world she imagines escaping the squalor of her existence and going abroad to Europe, where the height of wealth is celebrated. She tells Wesley, "They have everything in Europe. High art. Paintings. Castles. Buildings. Fancy food" (143).

Ella foolishly believes she can rise above her social class by selling the house and its small farm to Taylor, a land developer, but Wesley knows better. "You won't even make enough to take a trip to San Diego off this house. It's infested with termites," he tells her (146). Ella wants to get in on the expansion of the cities into the rural counties, something that Wesley sees as anathema. He tells Emma that his concern supersedes worries about what might happen to the family: he does not want to contribute to the slow suburbanization of the American landscape. His fear is not ecocritical in nature; rather he expresses his anxiety in language that recalls class warfare: "It means more than losing a house. It means losing a country. . . . It is a zombie invasion. Taylor is the head zombie. He's the scout for the other zombies. He's only a sign that more zombies are on their way. . . . There'll be bulldozers crashing through the orchard. There'll be giant steel balls crashing through the walls. There'll be foreman with their sleeves rolled up and blueprints under their arms. . . . Cement pilings. Prefab walls. Zombie architecture, owned by invisible zombies, built by zombies for the use and convenience of all zombies. A zombie city! Right here! Right where we're living now" (163). Embedded within Wesley's concern over the loss of his house is the gradual usurpation of the land by the ever-encroaching white upper class, whom Wesley compares to mindless zombies. Taylor, the land developer, sees the situation differently. As someone who can make money off the land, he sees the "opportunity" in the property as a civic duty to American's citizens: "Simple mathematics. More people demand more shelter. More shelter demands more land. It's an equation. . . . We're lucky to live in a country where that provision is possible" (153).

While Wesley is upset about the possible destruction of his childhood home, he reacts more to his mother's usurpation of his father's position as the head of the house. Sure enough, Weston shows up with his own idea of how to make money off his land, and just as Wesley predicts, he becomes enraged when he learns of the plan Ella has to sell the house to a land developer. He turns not just on Ella but on the entire family, proclaiming, "I'M BEING TAKEN FOR A RIDE BY EVERY ONE OF YOU! I'm the one who works! I'm the one who brings home food! THIS IS MY HOUSE! I BOUGHT THIS HOUSE! AND I'M SELLING THIS HOUSE! AND I'M TAKING ALL THE MONEY BECAUSE IT'S OWED ME!" (169). Even though Weston has the same idea as Ella, Wesley cannot quarrel with him; as the main authority figure of the house, Weston's decisions are beyond the realm of discussion from the other family members.

Shepard's exploration of the trope of food also expresses anxieties over the family's social class. In much the same way Shepard deciphers the mystery of gender identity as an inherent and inescapable curse, he also deconstructs the disconnection between social identity and class consciousness. Both Wesley and Emma know that they are not wealthy, but they cling to the notion that they are not poor; both children use the idea of food as proof of their social status. Early in the play Emma speaks to the refrigerator soothingly, as though a mother to her child: "Any corn muffins in there? Hello! Any produce? Any rutabagas? Any root vegetables? Nothing? It's all right. You don't have to be ashamed. I've had worse. I've had to take my lunch to school wrapped in a Weber's bread wrapper. That's the worst. Worse than no lunch. So don't feel bad! You'll get some company before you know it! You'll get some little eggs tucked into your sides and some yellow margarine tucked into your little drawers and some frozen chicken" (150). Emma understands that she is different from the other children when she brings her lunch wrapped in a bread wrapper, but she is optimistic that the family will soon prove their social status by filling the refrigerator.

As the main providers of the family, the only people who stock the refrigerator are Weston and Ella, the father and mother. When Weston comes home after his drinking binge, he has a sack full of artichokes that Wesley later boils. When Ella returns home after her night out with Taylor, she symbolically usurps Weston's control by throwing out the artichokes and stocking the fridge with groceries: "It's a joke bringing artichokes back here when we're out of food" (171). Throughout the play, all members of the family check the refrigerator constantly, as though affirming their social status through the amount of food in it. The hunger inside each family member, however, comes not strictly from a physical need for food, but from a metaphorical hunger that keeps them unsatisfied with their position in the family and their social class. When Wesley finds no food in the fridge, he tells the sick lamb he has been rehabilitating in the kitchen, "You're lucky I'm not really starving. You're lucky this is a civilized household. You're lucky it's not Korea and the rains are pouring through the cardboard walls and you're tied to a log in the mud and you're drenched to the bone and you're skinny and starving, but it makes no difference because someone's starving more than you. Someone's hungry. And his hunger takes him outside with a knife and slits your throat and eats you raw. His hunger eats you, and you're starving" (156). Wesley's appeal to the lamb reminds the audience that hunger remains a family identity; it represents their consistent dissatisfaction with their place in the social structure. Hunger references the inescapable ladders of the social hierarchy that cannot be overcome by get-rich-quick schemes. Though the family is poor, Wesley reminds himself that there are always people poorer, hungrier, and their predicament satisfies his desire to remain above "the starving class."

Later, at the end of the play, Wesley does indeed take the lamb out and slaughter it. Coming back into the house with its blood on his hands, Weston confronts him with his ironic action in a house full of food: "WHAT'D YA BUTCHER THE DUMB THING FOR! . . . THE ICE BOX IS CRAMMED FULL A' FOOD" (191). Wesley's initial explanation for slaughtering the lamb is that the family needs food, but Shepard's stage directions show that Wesley has turned to an almost bestial state, like a coyote (also a persistent trope throughout many of Shepard's plays): "Wesley crosses quickly to the refrigerator, opens it, and starts pulling all kinds of food out and eating it ravenously." The more Wesley eats, the less satisfied he is; he "keeps eating, throwing half-eaten food to one side and then digging into more. He groans slightly as he eats" (192). By the end of the act, Wesley has stooped to picking "scraps of food up off the floor" like an animal. Filling his body with food does nothing to change Wesley's identity. He is still his father's son and still a part of the "starving class" despite his efforts to escape, and his figurative hunger cannot be satiated by eating.

Divining the Cure

Shepard's initial exploration of the mystery of identity expands into the ways in which certain markers of identification can be read as curses. Wesley and Emma do not get to decide what family they are born into, what gender they are, what parents they will have, or what their social status might be. These crucial decisions, which will later define their identities, are out of their control and exist despite any discrepancies between how both are perceived or how they feel. Shepard explores the idea of "the curse" of identity through the image of the diseased lamb that appears in the first two acts of the play. In act 1 we learn that the lamb has been infected with maggots, and Wesley decides that the best place to "cure" him is in the kitchen, "the warmest part of the house" (155).

When Weston arrives home drunk, the lamb's presence confuses him; it violates his idea of what a house is supposed to be: a space of protection and domesticity. The lamb disrupts the familiarity of that space and negates the notion of the home itself. He asks the lamb, "Is this inside or outside? This is inside, right? This is the inside of the house. Even with the door out it's still the inside" (156). Placing the diseased lamb in the middle of the family's space provides an objective correlative for the curse of the family itself: that it violates a sense of the traditional ideas associated with family, such as peace, harmony, comfort, and protection.

As a symbol of the family's sickness, the lamb's health is debated by each family member. Weston first suggests healing the infected animal with chemicals: "Put some a' that blue shit on it. That'll fix him up. You know that blue stuff in the bottle?" (159). However, the lamb never does heal completely. Though Wesley initially plans on healing the animal in the kitchen, Ella and Emma both insist that he leave the lamb outside where it belongs. However, in the final act Weston brings the animal back into the kitchen in order to cure him for good. As the act opens, he speaks to the animal about being infected with parasites and notes that a physical ailment is preferable to the figurative curse afflicting the family: "There's worse things than maggots, ya' know. Much worse. Maggots go away if they're properly attended to" (182).

At the same time he plans on curing the lamb, Weston initiates a plan to cure himself and, by extension, his family of the soul sickness from which they suffer. He starts by reminding himself who he is fundamentally: "So I came back in here, and the first thing I did was I took all my old clothes off and walked around here naked. Just walked through the whole dam house in my birthday suit. Tried to get the feeling of it really being me in my house. . . . Then I walked straight in and made myself a hot bath. Hot as I could stand it. Just sank down into it and let it sink deep into the skin. Let it fog up all the windows and the glass on the medicine cabinet. Then I let all the water drain out, and then I filled it with ice cold water. Just sat there and let it creep up on me until I was up to my neck" (185). The cleansing ceremony works for Weston, who feels like a brand new man. Surprisingly he moves from being the site of authority in the house into an ambiguously gendered and subordinate role. He decides to do the family's laundry, a task he previously argued was the sole responsibility of Ella. Doing the laundry strangely connects Weston to the family: "And I felt like I knew every single one of you. Every one. Like I knew you through the flesh and blood. Like our bodies were connected and we could never escape."

It is in the act of doing the laundry that Weston has an epiphany that cures him of his desire to escape the suffocating family life. He finds that "it was good to be connected by blood like that. That a family wasn't just a social thing. It was an animal thing. It was a reason of nature that we were all together under the same roof. Not that we had to be but that we were supposed to be" (186). By moving through the various roles within the family—father, mother, son, daughter—Weston finds a connection that he has missed throughout his life. He does not want to escape the world of family life, and he relinquishes his role as the pinnacle of masculinity. At the same time, he acknowledges that his connection to his family is deeper than their social or familial identities, that it goes to something fundamental in who they are. There is a peace in his revelation, and, for the first time, he is eager to share something with his son.

He tells a bruised and battered Wesley (who has been beaten, ironically, attempting to get Weston's money back from Ellis) to follow in his footsteps: take a bath, put on new clothes, and, Weston assures the boy, he will feel the same connection to his own identity and the family that Weston himself has experienced. While Wesley attempts to take his father's "cure," Ella enters exhausted from a night at the police station with Emma. Though Weston and Ella quarrel, he eventually charms her into sleeping on the table while he prepares the family breakfast. In a strange reversal, Weston and Ella have regressed into children's roles at the same time that Wesley and Emma become the sites of authority in the house. Shepard signals a change in roles when Wesley enters naked from his bath and takes the lamb offstage to slaughter it. Similarly, when Emma returns, she comes back as a fierce gunfighter, an Annie Oakley figure boiling with the potential for violence.

Clearly Wesley's attempt to cure himself with his father's methodical ceremony does not work. He slaughters the lamb in a scene heavy with symbolism. Though he signals that he killed the lamb for food, Shepard suggests that the lamb itself is a sacrificial slaughter, Wesley's attempt to cure himself from his soul sickness. He tells Emma, "I tried his remedy but it didn't work. . . . I tried taking a hot bath. Hot as I could stand it. Then freezing cold. Then walking around naked. But it didn't work. Nothing happened. I was waiting for something to happen. I went outside. I was freezing cold out there and I looked for something to put over me. I started digging around in the garbage and I found his clothes. . . . I had the lamb's blood dripping down my arms. I thought it was me for a second. I thought it was me bleeding" (195). Wesley's final meditation on his sacrifice of the lamb connects all the identities Shepard has interrogated throughout *Curse of the Starving Class*. Wesley attempts to revise his role in the family through the symbolic act of violence. In slaughtering the lamb, he experiences not a surge of masculinity, but a strange connection to the feminine, a point made clear by the recollection of his sister's menstruation and his confusion over the lamb's blood and his own. His cure fails. Unlike his father, Wesley cannot "undo" his identity; he cannot take on other roles successfully. And just as he cannot learn masculinity from his father, the old man's suggestions on how to cure himself of the disease of identity do not work. Critic William Kleb argued that, though Wesley puts on his father's clothes, "the reversal . . . is an illusion . . . the transformation is a mirage, a masquerade, the latest and greatest of Weston's delusionary dreams."[23] Wesley has achieved nothing from either his father's cure or the purposeful attempt to become his father through the act of putting on his clothes.

The play ends on a fundamentally pessimistic note. While Weston acknowledges that family does not have to be a curse, that it can transcend its social definitions and can offer the opportunity to experiment with relationships, the play does not end with that hopeful epiphany. It ends with the old man's absence, a permanent state for fathers in the Shepard plays that follow. Weston is forced to flee for Mexico to hide from the loan sharks, and Emma is killed when the car she takes to escape is blown up by Emerson and Slater. In the final scene Wesley and Ella are left alone onstage without any idea of how to move forward without Weston. Significantly Wesley faces away from his mother as she speaks to him, indicating that, though they share a space together, they do not share any connection. In a final moment together, they try to piece together what little they can about the mystery of their identities through Weston's old stories. But there is, ultimately, no conclusion. The powerful ending reverberates through the action and central relationships among mother, father, and son in Shepard's next play, *Buried Child*.

CHAPTER 4

Hidden Trespasses
Buried Child

Whether or not he intended to, Shepard began his next play with a family that very much mirrored the one in *Curse of the Starving Class*. His new three-act family drama took the desperate and lonely final tableau between Wesley and Ella and transformed it into a starting place for a much bleaker exploration of the secret life of the American family. *Buried Child* imagines the slow dissolution of the family from the inside, not because of the external forces weighing on them. There are no loan sharks, land developers, and bar owners to threaten the existence of the family; instead the struggle to hide the family's dark past becomes the motivating factor that binds the members to each other. Ultimately, the play posits, such a shared burden cannot serve as the sole bond for family, and the play ends with their secrets compromised.

In *Curse of the Starving Class*, Shepard's aesthetic was rooted more in realism than in expressionism, and that is also true of *Buried Child*. The sparse kitchen of the earlier play is replaced by a much fuller and more complete set, with Shepard providing details about the set pieces: "Old wooden staircase . . . with pale, frayed carpet laid down on the steps . . . dark green sofa with the stuffing coming out in spots." The setting mirrors the family, which, once prosperous and close, has begun to unravel. In front of the sofa is "a large, old-fashioned brown T.V." with no picture save "a flickering blue light." In the back of the sofa is "a large, screened-in porch with a board floor." Like the house they live in, the family is slowly decaying. The elderly father of the family is dressed in a "well worn T-shirt" and draped himself in "an old brown blanket." The play opens with the image of the old man, "sickly looking"[1] and surreptitiously drinking a bottle of whiskey that he has hidden inside the cushions of the dilapidated sofa. From the characters to the setting, *Buried Child* easily contains the most realistic set that Shepard had written to this point.

Though the family exists in a naturalistic and representational space, the cohesion of the straightforward setting is gradually undercut by a complicated plot. At first the play's action seems conventional and linear, but by act 2, it flirts with the world of the absurd through some overwhelming and intense emotional moments. The play opens on a rain-drenched morning in the Illinois home of a dying patriarch, Dodge, who, throughout act 1, is harassed from offstage by his wife, Halie, about taking his medicine. During their conversation Halie antagonizes Dodge with memories of her secret affairs and old flames until their oldest son, Tilden, comes in from the storm muddied and carrying an armful of corn. Through the dialogue between Tilden and Dodge, we learn that Tilden has been in some sort of trouble in New Mexico and has returned to the family farm in Illinois because he cannot be trusted alone. Despite his father's claim otherwise, Tilden insists that the corn he is now shucking came from the family's crop, even though Dodge and Halie both insist that nothing has grown on their land since 1935. When Halie leaves to see Father Dewis about erecting a statue in honor of her deceased youngest son, Ansel, Dodge begs Tilden to stay with him in case Bradley, his middle child, comes to cut his hair. When Dodge falls asleep, however, Tilden steals his whiskey and covers him in the discarded corn husks. Alone, Dodge passes out long enough for Bradley, who is an amputee, to enter and cut his hair.

The second act opens with Vincent, Tilden's son, surprising the family on his way to visit his father, who he assumes still lives in New Mexico. He has brought along his girlfriend, Shelly, to meet everyone, but they are both stunned when they arrive and Dodge does not recognize him. While trying to come to terms with the idea that his grandfather has lost all knowledge of him, Vince is further distraught by the arrival of his father, this time carrying an armful of carrots that he picked from the supposedly barren family farm. As he tries to make some meaningful connections with his father and grandfather, Vince all but abandons Shelly to Tilden, who bonds with her by asking if she might clean the carrots he has brought in for supper. Shelly and Vince are both upset by Tilden's detached and emotionless personality. Despite Shelly's desperate attempts to get him to stay, Vince leaves her alone with Dodge and Tilden so that he can buy his grandfather a new bottle of whiskey. Alone with Tilden, Shelly learns a dark family secret involving Dodge's drowning of Tilden's first son, a revelation that quickly draws the ire of Dodge, who screams at his son to keep quiet. After Tilden's confession,

Bradley enters and frightens them both before sticking his fingers in Shelly's mouth in a strange attempt to manifest some kind of sexual power over the girl.

The final act begins with a sleeping Bradley, his wooden leg propped up against his head. Shelly and Dodge have a calm talk that is interrupted by a drunk Father Dewis and Halie. Because she has not met Shelly, Halie considers Shelly a stranger and asks her to leave the house. Dodge then reprimands Halie and airs the family secret he has kept for so long: he explains how Halie had a child long after he had stopped sleeping with her. Because Tilden cared for the baby so much, Dodge assumed he was the father and murdered it to protect the family's reputation. In the middle of the confusion and shock, Vince reenters the picture; he has been drinking all night and is still quite drunk. While he rants and raves about his place in the family, Dodge acknowledges that he is dying and gradually bequeaths various parts of his material inheritance to the family, leaving the house to Vince. One by one, each character exits the stage: Father Dewis leaves claiming that he did not know the family was in such a crisis; Halie retreats upstairs to escape the confrontations; Bradley chases his wooden leg offstage, where Vince has thrown it; and Shelly bids good-bye to her boyfriend as she escapes back to her home. Only Vince and Dodge (who has quietly passed away) remain on the sofa. As Vince talks to himself and Halie addresses her dead husband from upstairs, a muddy Tilden enters from the field and walks up the stairs toward his mother. In his hands he carries the bones of what the audience assumes is their murdered child.

Despite the play's realistic setting, Shepard's content might conceivably be classified as melodrama. The stakes in the play are unbelievably high, and Shepard does not bother to tie up the loose ends for the audience: What happened to Tilden in New Mexico? Why does Dodge refuse to acknowledge that Vince is his grandson? Where does Tilden get the bounty of crops that appear miraculously in his hands each time he enters the scene? Who fathered the "buried child," and why did Dodge decide to murder it? All these questions remain unanswered despite the audience's confrontation with the child's corpse. Nothing is resolved, and there is no tidy ending. The secrets of the family's past hang over the play like a dark cloud that threatens to annihilate the family's existence, and each member viciously attacks anyone who tries to expose any piece of information that might bring dishonor or shame to the family's place in the town.

Buried Child begins from the end point of *Curse of the Starving Class*, presenting a family cursed by its own history. The setting of the house and Dodge's clothes both show the family's gradual decay and decline. Halie and

Dodge are shocked when Tilden brings in fresh produce from the field where nothing has grown in over forty years: even the land itself seems cursed by the family's secrets. Once prosperous and honorable, the family has become poor and pitiable. Tilden was once a great football player, and Dodge and Halie were once pillars of the community. Now, however, the family has become social pariahs. Despite Halie's attempts to raise their social status by celebrating their youngest son, who, like Tilden, was also a sports star and hero, Father Dewis becomes privy to the terrifying news of Dodge's infanticide. Like Weston and Ella, Dodge and Halie cannot rise above the community's negative perception of them; they cannot become the family they want to be; in large part this is because of their formidable history and secret sins.

Inside the family there is also a clear struggle over defining one's power in relation to masculinity. When Tilden returns from New Mexico, he is shell shocked and broken. At the mercy of his father's pronouncements, he can assert his power only when Dodge sleeps. Similarly Bradley accepts his place within the family as subservient to Dodge's masculinity. It is only when the old man sleeps that he can assert his control over his father through the symbolic act of cutting his hair. Without his leg, Bradley is a simpering and powerless child in the family; he is unable to control anything or exert his power over anyone. Vince arrives in the midst of the power struggle over masculinity and, initially, does not participate. However, by the end of the play, he has cemented himself as the new font of masculine power inside the house. Recognizing Vince's new authority, Dodge bequeaths the property to the boy as his final act.

While *Buried Child* plays with the idea of inheritance through Dodge's decision to give the land to Vince, it also explores *Curse of the Starving Class*'s emphasis on the emotional inheritance passed on from father to son. Just as Wesley cannot escape the sins of Weston, Dodge's sons are all damaged by his decision to murder Halie's illicit child. Perhaps because the dead child's father is unknown (and thus out of the closed circle of the family), or perhaps because the child is the result of an incestuous relationship between Halie and one of her sons, Dodge's act of murder can be read as a refusal to acknowledge the baby as a member of the family he heads. As the sole pillar of masculine authority in the house, his decision to murder the child, however, dooms the family to a lifetime of misery. Unable to exist simultaneously with the modern world outside their home, the members of the family instead draw in more tightly until their relationships become suffocating. No one in the family can escape Dodge's action, and because of it, they are forced into inaction and despair.

Shepard's title itself seems to reference the final tableau of the play, with Tilden edging closer and closer to his mother's bedroom where he will confront her with the physical evidence of Dodge's horrific action. But the final scene remains purposefully ambiguous: is Shepard optimistic that a physical confrontation with the sins of the past will be the miracle that will lift the curse of Dodge's crime? Now that Dodge has passed away, can the family find its footing through recognition of its sins? Or is Shepard suggesting that Tilden's presentation of the corpse to Halie represents the final, vicious circle of the family's decline? By confronting his mother with the evidence of the family's ruin, can Tilden transform Halie's perspective and thereby introduce the possibility of saving the family from itself? The answers to these questions remain as mysterious and hidden as the location of the child's body. By not offering an easy answer, Shepard has left the family's emotional inheritance and how it will affect future generations an even deeper mystery.

Production History

The first performance of *Buried Child* was at San Francisco's Magic Theatre in the summer of 1978. Robert Woodruff, who had directed Shepard's *Curse of the Starving Class* for its New York premiere, directed the first cast. Woodruff's run went so well in California that Shepard tapped him to direct the play's New York premiere, at Theater for the New City. The initial run lasted only three weeks, but Shepard's new play was a true hit: it would continue to run for four months at the bohemian Theatre de Lys in Greenwich Village. Don Shewey called the Woodruff run "the single best production of a Shepard play that had yet been seen in New York."[2] A day after it closed, Shepard received word that he had won the Pulitzer Prize for Drama. Buoyed by a new interest in his work, the play reopened at the Circle Repertory Theater and ran until September, bringing the total run of the play to almost a full year.

Reviewers of the play in 1979 were uniformly positive about Shepard's deepening exploration of the mythos surrounding the American family. But perhaps the biggest excitement in the history of the production of *Buried Child* came in a revival. In the late 1990s Chicago's acclaimed Steppenwolf Theatre, which had "reversed public opinion on *True West*"[3] with its 1983 production with Gary Sinise and John Malkovich, mounted a revival of the Pulitzer Prize–winning play with well-known stage actors James Gammon and Lois Smith as the parents as well as the young film actor Ethan Hawke as Vince. As the rehearsals began, director Gary Sinise was shocked to find that Shepard was giving him rewrites. More than fifteen years after he had won the most respected award in American theater, Shepard was changing his play in a fundamental way.

The 1997 Steppenwolf Revision

In an interview in September 1996 with Stephanie Coen, Shepard addressed the reason behind his desire to rewrite the show. When he approached the play years later, Shepard found weaknesses throughout the play that culminated in a heaviness he had tried to avoid: "You see the weaknesses, and one of the weaknesses is that Vince hasn't been fully explored. For one thing, the old man was a lot more fun. I could really go with him, but the kid wasn't so much fun. Now the kid is starting to become more and more apparent to me. . . . I geared the play towards this humor, because I felt that the play in our first production was too heavy. There's a lot of humor in it—mainly based on Dodge's kind of out-of-the-side-of-the-mouth humor, his sarcasm, that strange World War II humor—that I wanted to emphasize. I think the play works because the audience is allowed into this strange kind of humor in spite of themselves."[4] When the revival (and revision) premiered in Chicago, interest in the play was so huge that a decision was made to try to move the production to Broadway, a first in Shepard's career. The play, staged this time at the Brooks Atkinson Theatre, was a hit all over again. *New York Times* critic Ben Brantley raved that the play "operates successfully on so many levels that you get dizzy watching it. It has the intangible spookiness of nightmares about home and dispossession, yet it involves you in its tawdry, mystery-driven plot with the old-fashioned verve of an Erskine Caldwell novel."[5] In the eyes of audiences and theater critics, *Buried Child* had finally received a production worthy of its importance.

But for literary critics, a new revision of such a revered text was shocking: Shepard's original 1977 script for *Buried Child* had appeared on stages for approximately twenty years, and now the playwright had decided to tinker with his most famous play for a revival at Chicago's Steppenwolf Theatre? Though the performances took place in 1996, the revision was not published until 1997 by Dramatists Play Service, and the publication still remains a hotly debated matter among Shepard scholars. The new text stood as something of an anomaly for a writer who does not often revise a piece after it has been performed. The core of the revisions involves clearing up the mystery of the titular infant of the play. While the original version of *Buried Child* leaves the parentage of the murdered child something of a puzzle, Shepard virtually erases any doubt in his new script that the baby, indeed, belongs to Tilden and Halie.

The revisions come at key moments in the script: when either Tilden or Dodge mentions the particulars of the child that Dodge has murdered and buried somewhere on the family's land. For example, a conversation between Dodge and Halie initially read

DODGE: My flesh and blood's buried in the back yard!
HALIE: That's enough, Dodge. (77)

However, in his Steppenwolf revision, Shepard added a line after Halie's admonition; she now says, "You've become confused."[6] Later in the revised version, Tilden questions Dodge about his comment: "Why'd you tell her it was *your* flesh and blood?"[7] These additions seek to eliminate the possibility that Dodge was the father of the baby, and thus clarify the fact of Tilden's incestuous moment with his mother. The revisions also delay the revelation of the murder until the beginning of act 3, a move that critic James Stacy has noted makes dramatic sense as "the impact of the confession is maximized."[8] No longer does Tilden accidentally blurt out the truth of the murder to Shelly in act 2; instead Dodge's confession is presented in a brutally honest monologue to the girl. Literary scholars decried the changes as nothing less than the elimination of the crux of *Buried Child*; however, Shepard explained to Stephanie Coen that he "didn't want anything in the play to be gratuitously mysterious. And I felt that certain questions that were ignited in the play should find—not resolution, they shouldn't be resolved—but they should be at least followed through."[9]

While Tilden's role in the confession is minimized, in the revisions Tilden has "gained twice as many words as he has lost."[10] Similarly Vince loses few lines, and the ones he has expand, thus cementing him as the main character of the play. Shepard added new dialogue surrounding the young man's shock at not being recognized by his family. The playwright also clarified the relationship between Father Dewis and Halie as a romantic one. When Dodge speaks about Halie's night out in act 2, he says, "Halie is out with her boyfriend. The Right Reverend Dewis. He's not a breeder-man but a man of God."[11] Stacy has noted that Shepard also "intensifies Bradley's weakness to the point of total emasculation"[12] by eliminating most of his lines in act 3 and acknowledging the extreme helplessness the loss of his leg brings him.

While the revisions are not extensive, they do offer a different perspective on the actions of the family in *Buried Child*. Critics have debated whether Shepard's work on the play almost twenty years after its initial premiere represents a deepening of the original message or whether it presents more problems than it solves. With respect to the central question of the title, many critics argue that "solving" the puzzle through the purposeful addition of Dodge's confession might eliminate confusion over a key plot point, but it also eradicates possible meanings and concerns that might have served the play better. Part of the mystery of *Buried Child* comes from the inability to know with certainty all the family's secrets. Critic James Stacy has argued that "the question [of the buried child's paternity] may have been richer in the shadows of ambiguity."[13] In short, not knowing the truth seems to be one of the central tropes Shepard explores throughout both the play and his oeuvre, and many critics felt that his decision to make the truth plain mitigates the impact of this in the revised version. It did, however, make the play easier to understand and much easier to market to a larger audience. The revised *Buried Child* that premiered at Steppenwolf later became Shepard's first play to run on Broadway.

Professional and Personal Influences

Like *Curse of the Starving Class*, *Buried Child* is a play deeply rooted in Shepard's life. Don Shewey has argued, "The two plays are clearly companion pieces. . . . *Curse* seems like the warm-up in that it takes place on two distinct planes, one poetic . . . the other narrative. . . . *Buried Child* is paradoxically both more conventional and more original" (119). Clearly *Buried Child* carries with it the ghosts of Shepard's old works: "all the way back to the woman's one-sided conversation in *The Rock Garden*. The familiar yet stylized domestic activity recalls *Action*, the overlapping realities *Suicide in B-flat*, the flying veggies *Curse of the Starving Class*."[14] *Buried Child*'s originality comes in the synthesis of all these familiar Shepard moments within the context of a darkly comic and absurd reflection on the breakdown of the American family.

Besides engaging with Shepard's own work, *Buried Child* also borrows from the works of other dramatists. There are marked similarities between the plot and action of *Buried Child* and Harold Pinter's *The Homecoming*, but critics compare Shepard's play most often with Henrik Ibsen's *Ghosts*. Both Don Shewey and Thomas Adler have commented on the critical connection between the final moments of *Ghosts* and *Buried Child*. When Halie notices the miracle of the crop in the once-dead field, she postulates, "Maybe it's the sun" that has broken the curse. The significance of the pun is obvious to the audience, who in a moment of absolute dramatic irony watch Halie's son Tilden carrying a baby (also Halie's "son") upstairs for a final confrontation. Similarly, at the end of Ibsen's *Ghosts*, Oswald Alving exclaims, "The sun—the sun," to his mother as he asks for relief from a debilitating affliction. Adler concluded that the connection between Shepard and Ibsen's pun lies in a similar semantic meaning: "the audience hears both 'sun' and 'son.'"[15] Adler noted, too, that the structure of the plays is similar: "both build to the revelation of an awful secret . . . the set for each play includes a variation on the inner stage . . . beyond which the rain falls in the first two acts of each." The plot of *Ghosts* also follows a young man who returns to the home of his ancestors only to find "the biological bond [does not] necessarily guarantee love." Whether or not Shepard meant to reference Ibsen—an author whom, according to biographer Don Shewey, he claims never to have read[16]—critics have maintained that *Buried Child* draws from Ibsen's work.

Buried Child also contains elements of the works of the playwright Eugene O'Neill, especially of his *Desire under the Elms* and *Long Day's Journey into Night*. The stage directions at the opening of *Buried Child* note that beyond the house are "dark elm trees" (63), a reference Bert Cardullo has found an explicit reminder of O'Neill's play, "which, like Shepard's, focuses on a father-son rivalry and one son's desire to claim his inheritance."[17] Beyond basic plot points, critic Lauren Porter has noted that Shepard's *Buried Child* and O'Neill's *Long Day's Journey into Night* both share "cyclical structures, with final scenes that become ironic mockeries of their opening episode."[18] However, Porter concluded that the "parallels . . . between these two dramas, abundant though they are, ultimately reveal vast differences in their philosophical underpinnings," with O'Neill presenting "lost souls seeking a salvation forever beyond their grasp" and Shepard exploring " a family so fragmented and action so driven by random and inexplicable events that the very quest itself seems absurd."[19]

Shepard has also used the play to explore myths and legends, including the myth of Osiris and the biblical story of the prodigal son. However, according to Cardullo, "there are two prodigal sons" in Shepard's text: "Tilden, who has returned to the family after twenty years of doing nothing in New Mexico and Vince, who is a virtual stranger to his father."[20] Cardullo went on to argue that by putting on Dodge's decaying blanket after the old man's death, Shepard means to reference "the fine robe" of the biblical prodigal son. Shepard's continued references to the dead field outside producing miraculous crops also seems to be based on "the myth of Osiris . . . [who] was slain by a jealous brother who dismembered the body and scattered its remains throughout the arid Nile Valley, which mysteriously became fertile whenever it held pieces of Osiris's corpse."[21] Tilden, in a moment that recalls the myth of Osiris, finds a pocket of fertile growth in the once-dead fields, and only at the end, does the audience realize this fecund spot holds the corpse of his murdered child. By engaging throughout his text with his own autobiography, other playwrights, myth, legends, and existing dramatic structures, Shepard has renegotiated the space of dramatic ritual and transformed *Buried Child* into a play with connections across multiple cultures, texts, and philosophies.

Miracles and Curses

Buried Child begins with an exploration of the trope of the "curse" similar to the one that permeated *Curse of the Starving Class;* but the consequences of the curse that befalls the family in *Buried Child* appear to be much more literal than the psychological ennui experienced in his earlier play. While Wesley and Emma attempted to overcome the curse of their familial and gendered identities, the characters in *Buried Child* seem to deal with a much more mystical curse that has physical consequences. Early in the play Shepard's setting signals that the family seems to be decaying: the sofa is falling apart; Dodge's clothes look as though they have rotted on his skin; and the television projects nothing but a flickering, blue color. Halie admonishes her husband that he looks as though he is dying; she says, "You sit here day and night, festering away! Decomposing! Smelling up the house with your putrid body!" (76). As the audience enters into this world, almost as if into a fairy tale, the very stage is littered with remnants of the family's past that have continued to exist despite their decay.

Just as the family decays, the very land itself seems to be rotting away. When Tilden enters in act 1 carrying an armload of corn, Dodge interrogates him about where he picked the ears, unwilling to believe that his abandoned fields could have produced such a harvest:

DODGE: Where'd you pick it from?
TILDEN: Right out back.
DODGE: Out back where?
TILDEN: Right out in back.
DODGE: There's nothing out there!
TILDEN: There's corn.
DODGE: There hasn't been corn out there since about nineteen thirty-five.
    That's the last time I planted corn out there!
TILDEN: It's out there now. (69)

As Tilden begins shucking his new corn, Halie and Dodge both worry that he has stolen the crop from a neighboring farm; neither can accept their son's assertion that their fruitless soil produced anything so abundant.

Even so, Dodge marvels at the beauty of the corn and wonders aloud if it is "some kind of fancy hybrid" (71). His assertion that the corn might be a "hybrid" growing in the useless soil of his land anticipates the possible source of the "miraculous" growth and the play's title: the decomposing body of Tilden and Halie's child in the field, itself a hybrid offspring of mother and son. However, because Tilden has not yet unearthed the body, the miracle remains a puzzle for him. When Halie asks him the loaded question, "What is the meaning of this corn Tilden!" he responds, "It's a mystery to me. I was out back there. And the rain was coming down. And I didn't feel much like coming back inside. I didn't feel the cold so much. I didn't mind the wet. So I was just walking. I was muddy but I didn't mind the mud so much. And I looked up. And I saw this stand of corn. In fact I was standing in it. So, I was standing in it. . . . I didn't steal it" (75–76). The mystery of the corn immediately becomes connected with the mysterious secret the family hides: seconds after Halie's interrogation of Tilden, Dodge spits out, "My flesh and blood's buried in the back yard" (77), causing the entire family to "freeze" in their tracks. Shepard's connecting of the two mysteries of the play—the miracle of the invisible harvest and the hidden secret of the buried child—signals that neither major puzzle can be solved without the other.

When Tilden reappears in act 2, he holds a new harvest, an armful of carrots. Unresponsive to his son Vince, who thinks his father is still in New Mexico, he takes his crop to Vince's girlfriend, Shelly. With his hands full, he connects with her over the new vegetables he has found:

TILDEN: Back yard's full of carrots. Corn. Potatoes.
SHELLY: You're Vince's father, right?
TILDEN: All kinds of vegetables. You like vegetables?
SHELLY: (laughs) Yeah. I love vegetables.
TILDEN: We could cook these carrots ya' know. You could cut 'em up and we could cook 'em.
SHELLY: All right.
TILDEN: I'll get you a pail and a knife. . . . I'll be right back. Don't go. (93)

Just as before, the interaction with the miracle crop of carrots opens up a space for Tilden to speak about the child. Sitting with Shelly as she prepares the carrots for dinner, Tilden confesses portions of the family's secret. The interaction with the vegetables almost seems to break the curse of silence surrounding the family and allows Tilden to speak his secret.

By speaking about the truth that lays hidden in the fields behind the house, Tilden exorcises the demons that have haunted his father and—by extension—the entire family. Though he first believes she will not understand the story, Tilden confesses to Shelly portions of the secret of Dodge's crime: "We had a baby. He did. Dodge did. Could pick it up with one hand. Put it in the other. Little baby. Dodge killed it. . . . Never told Halie. Never told anybody. Just drowned it. . . . Nobody could find it. Just disappeared. Cops looked for it. Neighbors. Nobody could find it. . . . Finally everybody just gave up. Just stopped looking. Everybody had a different answer. Kidnap. Murder. Accident. Some kind of accident. . . . He's the only one who knows where it's buried. The only one. Like a secret buried treasure. Won't tell any of us" (103–4). Tilden's speech exposes the family's curse: the secret murder of a little child, and by speaking the sin out loud, Tilden finds a space for transformation. This suggests that unearthing the secret is the key to unlock the decay and despair under which the family exists.

It is significant that Tilden discovers the vegetables, for he is the one who engages in discourse about the past. He seems to understand implicitly that by speaking about the past, one can renegotiate its burden. Dodge, on the other hand, resists dwelling on the past. He lives in a continual present. When Shelly asks about the pictures of him as a young man hanging on the family's walls, he reacts angrily:

DODGE: That isn't me! That never was me! This is me. Right here. This is it. The whole shootin' match, sittin' right in front of you.
SHELLY: So the past never happened as far as you're concerned?
DODGE: The past? Jesus Christ. The past. What do you know about the past?
SHELLY: Not much. I know there was a farm.
DODGE: A farm?
SHELLY: There's a picture of a farm. A big farm. A bull. Wheat. Corn.
DODGE: Corn? (111)

The mention of the family farm (and specifically the crops that grew on it) reminds Dodge of the cyclical nature of humanity, how all things are reborn, but it reminds the audience of Tilden's act 1 unearthing of the miraculous corn and how it connects to Dodge's unspeakable act. Unable to confront his deed, Dodge retreats inside of himself. He chastises the girl for bringing up the past: "How far back can you go," he asks her, "A long line of corpses! There's not a living soul behind me. Not a one. . . . Who gives a damn about bones in the ground?" (112). His final question clearly reverberates onstage, as Tilden's confession about the buried child remains forefront in the minds of both the audience and Shelly, who asks, "Was Tilden telling the truth?"

Eventually Dodge confesses his crime to the girl and to Father Dewis, who has come home with a tipsy Halie. He tells the assembled family about the family's eventual decline because of his awful misdeed:

See, we were a well established family once. Well established. All the boys were grown. The farm was producing enough milk to fill Lake Michigan twice over. Me and Halie were pointed toward what looked like the middle part of our life. Everything was settled with us. All we had to do was ride it out. Then Halie got pregnant again. Outa' the middle of nowhere, she got pregnant . . . we hadn't been sleepin' in the same bed for about six years. . . . She had it. . . . It wanted to be just like us. It wanted to be a part of us. It wanted to pretend that I was its father. She wanted me to believe in it. Even when everyone around us knew. . . . Tilden was the one who knew. . . . We couldn't allow that to grow up right in the middle of our lives. It made everything we accomplished look like it was nothin'. Everything was cancelled out by this one mistake. This one weakness. . . . I killed it. I drowned it. Just like the runt of the litter. Just drowned it. (123–24)

Dodge's confession of the murder also contains within it the suggestion of incest, as he implicates Tilden as the father of the illicit child. The dual confessions unlock the secret of the family's curse: a curse born not simply from the murder of the baby, but from the hidden and dark incestuous moment between mother and son. Though once a "well established family," they have now become pariahs: Dodge literally decays throughout the play; Tilden is a shell of himself; and Halie exists mostly offstage, where she does not have to confront the family's secret sins. However, what was once hidden becomes exposed, and as their horrific secrets are aired to two strangers (Dewis and Shelly), the curse seems to lift.

The end of the play, with the confession of the family's secrets hanging over the audience, suggests that finally the demons of the past have been banished. As Tilden carries the newly unearthed bones of his murdered child up to his mother and lover, Halie remarks on the changes in the land: "Tilden was right about the corn you know. I've never seen such corn. Have you taken a look at it lately? Tall as a man already. This early in the year. Carrots too. Potatoes. Peas. It's like a paradise out there. . . . A miracle" (131). Finally the land has yielded to the confession of the secret. By speaking the sin to the world, the family can exist again. Significantly, as Tilden approaches an unsuspecting Halie with the once-hidden body of the murdered child, Halie praises the rain for its miraculous and mysterious way of making things grow: "You can't force a thing to grow. . . . It's all hidden. It's all unseen" (132), she remarks. Her declaration of the miracle of growth connects its power to its mystery: the process is hidden from anyone else. She ends her reverie (and Shepard ends the play) with the pun "Maybe it's the sun," suggesting that it is both the sun's rays that caused the crops to grow and the reclamation of her "son" from the ground that lifts the final curse.

"A stranger in my house": Family and Sites of Memory

One section of the play that Shepard felt he may have underdeveloped in the original production was Vince's outrage over being forgotten by his family. Instead of Vince—a clear stand-in for the young Shepard—being the central figure of the play, Dodge's presence had been the focus of the audience. Therefore Shepard reduced Dodge's lines and added several interactions between Vince and his family in the 1997 revisions. Perhaps Shepard felt so strongly about including more material about Vince's shock at being forgotten because the dual ideas of "stranger" and "family" are clearly central themes of the play. Even before Vince's arrival in act 2, Shepard examines the curious differences in Tilden's personality. Once a star athlete and a model son, Tilden's time in New Mexico changes him. He returns to the family as a different person: broken, hollow, shell shocked. Dodge tries to engage his son with an appeal to their relationship; "I'm still your father," he assures the man, and Tilden answers, "I know you're still my father" (70). And yet the fundamental relationship has been altered in a way inexplicable to the audience.

Halie, too, remarks on how Tilden has changed. She notices that he has retreated inward and become almost childlike after his experiences in New Mexico. She warns Dodge, "He can't look after himself anymore, so we have to do it. Nobody else will do it. We can't just send him away somewhere. . . . I was always hoping that Tilden would look out for Bradley when they got older. After Bradley lost his leg. Tilden's the oldest. I always thought he'd be the one to take responsibility. I had no idea in the world that Tilden would be so much trouble. Who would've dreamed. Tilden was an All-American, don't forget. Don't forget that. Fullback. Or quarterback. I forget which" (72). Shepard's humor is subtle throughout: though Halie warns Dodge not to forget who Tilden once was, she herself has already forgotten what position he played in high school. She also speaks to her husband as though Tilden were not in the room. Shepard's implication is clear: the man has become a stranger to his own family.

Forgetting the past becomes a theme that Shepard utilizes to comment on the purposeful break the family makes in meditating on their history. Tilden's admonition to his father regarding Dodge's mentioning of the dead baby to Halie underscores the ambiguity of Shepard's binaries of family/stranger and remembering/forgetting: "What difference does it make? Everybody knows, everybody's forgot" (77). Dodge's forced amnesia stems both from his hand in the murder of the illicit child and from the fact that he was not the father. Tilden goes further, suggesting that forgetting the child is especially difficult for Halie because she was the mother: "It's different for a woman," he tells Dodge. "She couldn't forget that. How could she forget that?" (78). As the matriarch of the family, Halie embodies the site of the family's memory, of what can be remembered and what can be forgotten.

Another central character who calls to mind the binary between remembering and forgetting is the youngest child, Ansel. Because Ansel is dead, his memory can be celebrated by Halie. To her, Ansel represents "a hero . . . a genuine hero. Brave. Strong. And very intelligent" (73). Although "he didn't die in action" the way a real war hero might have, Halie spends the entirety of the play preparing for and meeting with Father Dewis, a local priest. They debate "putting up a plaque for Ansel" or even "a big tall statue [of Ansel] with a basketball in one hand and a rifle in the other" (73). However, the family cannot even agree on who Ansel was. Bradley notes that his brother "never played basketball" (116), and no one can quite remember the boy like Halie and Dewis. "You remember," Halie tells Father Dewis about her son, "You remember how he could play" (117). To Halie, Ansel has ceased to be anything but a fantasy, an image fashioned by her selective memory of the past. While the rest of the family remembers a different Ansel, she alone claims authorship over his memory and even constructs a monument to who she believes he was.

In much the same way that Halie tries to force Dodge and Tilden to remember only good memories (or fantasies), Dodge tries to get Tilden to collaborate with him in a joyful collective memory from his past:

DODGE: You can watch the Red Sox. Pee Wee Reese. Pee Wee Reese. You remember Pee Wee Reese?

TILDEN: No.

DODGE: Was he with the Red Sox?

TILDEN: I don't know.

DODGE: Pee Wee Reese. You can watch the Cardinals. You remember Stan Musial.

TILDEN: No.

DODGE: Stan Musial. Bases loaded. Top a' the sixth. Bases loaded. . . . Ball just took off like a rocket. Just pulverized. I marked it. . . . First kid out there. First kid. I had to fight hard for that ball. I wouldn't give it up. They almost tore the ears right off me. But I wouldn't give it up. (80–81)

Though Dodge attempts to connect with his son, it is over a memory from Dodge's own childhood, not the boy's, a memory for which Tilden has no context or connection. Instead of connecting father and son, the memory isolates them until Dodge drifts off to sleep and Tilden steals his hidden bottle of whiskey. Attempting to remember collectively fails, distancing and separating father and son even further.

The space between forgetting and remembering becomes larger still when Vince arrives on his way to visit Tilden in New Mexico. As he enters the house and greets his grandfather, however, it is clear that no one remembers him. The inability of the family to remember Vince becomes the emotional crux of the play, and Shepard exploits it as a rhetorical marker indicating the family's inability to reconcile their collective past. When Vince and his girlfriend first arrive at the house, a nervous Shelly babbles compulsively to a near-comatose Dodge about why they have come: "We're going all the way through to New Mexico. To see his father. I guess his father lives out there. We thought we'd stop by and see you on the way. Kill two birds with one stone, you know? . . . I mean Vince has this thing about his family now. I guess it's a new thing with him. I kind of find it hard to relate to. But he feels it's important. You know. I mean he feels he wants to get to know you all again. After all this time" (86). Vince's desire to reconnect not only with his father but also with his grandfather, grandmother, and uncles seems to stem from a conscious acknowledgment on his part that—after so many years—he does not have a meaningful relationship with anyone in his family. He comes back to his father's home not simply to reestablish a connection with the family from whom he has grown apart, but also to use his relationships with them as a way to comprehend his own identity.

Vince's experiment fails terribly. Not only does Dodge not recognize his grandson, he proudly asserts that he has none: "I'm nobody's Grandpa" (90), he spits back at the young man. Shelly questions Vince about the strange reaction he receives from his own family:

SHELLY: Maybe you've got the wrong house. Did you ever think of that? Maybe this is the wrong address!
VINCE: It's not the wrong address! I recognize the yard.
SHELLY: Yeah but do you recognize the people? He says he's not your Grandfather. . . .
VINCE: He's just sick or something. I don't know what's happened to him. (90)

When his father arrives with an armful of vegetables, Vince cannot seem to get the man to recognize him either, in spite of Shelly's attempts to bring them together: "This is supposed to be your son," she says to Tilden. "Is he your son? Do you recognize him! . . . I thought everybody knew each other!" (92).

Though he comes home to reconnect with a family and an identity that he has not engaged in several years, Vince appears to be nothing more than a stranger to his family. At first he tries to convince Dodge and Tilden of their relationship by engaging in familiar actions: drumming on his teeth, bending back his knuckles, joking around by pretending to talk through his stomach. None of these attempts work, however, and Vince eventually blames himself ("Maybe it's me. Maybe I forgot something" [96] he says to Shelly). Gradually, though, Vince comes to the conclusion that the family's inability to recognize him might be part of an elaborate curse based on some inexplicable sin in his past: "Boy! This is amazing. This is truly amazing. . . . What is this anyway? Am I in a time warp or something? Have I committed an unpardonable offense? It's true, I'm not married. . . . But I'm also not divorced. . . . How could they not recognize me! How in the hell could they not recognize me! I'm their son!" (97). The curse hanging over the family's past seems to obliterate all memories of Vince. Dodge refuses to acknowledge his familial connection with the young man, and Tilden seems completely unaffected by Vince's attempts to remind him that he is his son.

While Vince is irate over his family's ignorance, Shelly is terrified. As a true stranger in the family's house, she remains even more remotely disconnected from Dodge and Tilden. When Vince tries to leave to clear his head and buy a bottle of whiskey for Dodge, Shelly begs him not to go:

SHELLY: Look, you think you're bad off, what about me? Not only don't they recognize me but I've never seen them before in my life. I don't know who these guys are. They could be anybody!

VINCE: They're not anybody!

SHELLY: That's what you say.

VINCE: They're my family for Christ's sake. I should know who my own family is! (97)

The play continues to reference the stranger/family binary and suggests that the breakdown of the family's relationships lies in their collective rejection of their shared past. Because they have sworn not to mention either the illicit child or Dodge's murder of it, they are unable to access even the slightest memory from their history. To Shelly, the family could be "anybody"; there is no context to suggest that they exist as Vince's family.

Though at first he is unrecognized, Vince's return to the family ignites the family's memories. Like the pictures on the wall, Vince becomes a site of memory for the family, and Tilden feels a connection that he expresses to Shelly: "I thought I recognized him. I thought I recognized something about him. . . . I thought I saw a face inside his face" (100). Buoyed by his new memories, Tilden is able to conjure the haunting memory that continues to curse the household and confess it to Shelly for the first time. By sharing "family business" with a stranger, the play conflates the binary between stranger/family and opens a space for the curse of silence to be exorcised. Tilden's confession becomes Shelly's initiation into the family, and by the third act she is speaking to Dodge as a member of the family. In her role as not-stranger and not-family, she tells the old man that, for a moment, she forgot she was not in her own house, that she had the feeling "that nobody lives here but me. I mean everybody's gone. . . . It's the house or something. Something familiar. Like I know the way around here" (110).

In her new position, Shelly interrogates Dodge about his past: "What's happened to this family anyway?" she asks powerfully (112). She wants to know everything about the children, about Halie and her secrets. Now that she has built a relationship with both Dodge and Tilden (and, to a lesser extent, Bradley, who forces himself on her in a bizarre show of power), Shelly still recognizes that she is not a part of the family. When Halie returns in act 3, the woman questions Shelly about her connection to Dodge and the family. When her answers are unacceptable, Shelly is once again outside the circle of the family. Halie remarks to Father Dewis, "Father, there's a stranger in my house. What would you advise? What would be the Christian thing?" (116).

Though Shelly is a "stranger" to Halie, the young woman continues to address the family as though they were her own. Gradually, however, she has to admit that, just as they do not recognize Vince, she cannot piece together the fantasy Vince created from the reality of the family in front of her: "You all say you don't remember Vince, okay, maybe you don't. Maybe it's Vince that's crazy. Maybe he's made this whole family thing up. I don't even care anymore. I was just coming along for the ride. I thought it'd be a nice gesture. Besides, I was so curious. He made you all sound so familiar to me. Every one of you. For every name, I had an image. Every time he'd tell me a name, I'd see the person. In fact, each of you was so clear in my mind that I actually believed it was you. I really believed that when I walked through that door the people who lived here would turn out to be the same people in my imagination. But I don't recognize any of you. Not one" (121). In an ironic reversal, Shelly—the stranger in the family's house—rejects Halie, Dodge, Tilden, and Bradley as the ultimate strangers. They do not resemble Vince's family, or any family, for that matter. They appear to her to be a loose group of strangers with no real connection to one another. That realization sparks another confession to a stranger, this time by Dodge to Father Dewis. It is this final confession (also, significantly, before a priest, a "Father") that seems finally to expel the curse hanging over the family: Dodge passes away, but before he does, he finally recognizes his grandson and bequeaths him his house.

Significantly, while Vince stays in the house as the new figurehead of masculine power (he tells Dewis, "This is my house now, ya' know? All mine" [131]), both the strangers—Father Dewis and Shelly—retreat into the darkness. When Shelly asks Vince to come with her, he declines, noting that during his trip last night, he had a meaningful epiphany on the responsibilities of family. While driving, Vince comes to the realization: "I could see myself in the windshield. My face. My eyes. I studied my face. Studied everything about it. As though I was looking at another man. As though I could see his whole race behind him. . . . And then his face changed. His face became his father's face. Same bones. Same eyes. Same nose. Same breath. And his father's face changed to his Grandfather's face. And it went on like that. Changing. Clear on back to faces I'd never seen before but still recognized. Still recognized the bones underneath. . . . I followed my family clear into Iowa. Every last one. Straight into the Corn Belt and further. Straight as far back as they'd take me" (130). Vince's powerful engagement with the importance of family recalls the binary of forgetting/remembering that Shepard used in act 1 to signal the usefulness of family. As a site of the family's memory, Vince becomes the repository for all of the family's past, good and bad, and within his singular persona exists the faces of all of his ancestors, "every last one."

No longer a stranger in his family's house, Vince transforms himself and the land: he becomes the head of power in his own house. The family's secrets have been exposed to strangers, and Dodge's death suggests that the curse that began with his murder of the illicit child has finally been lifted. In the final act of coming together as a family, Tilden ascends the staircase with the corpse of the now-unearthed child, a child that clearly belongs to both Halie and Tilden. As a final act the moment is fraught with ambiguity. Is it a confrontation? An invitation to remember? A mourning? A rebirth? Despite Shepard's lack of easy answers, one crucial part of Tilden's act is sure: his desire to share the child's body with his (and its) mother is an attempt to remember, to reclaim the baby as a member of the family.

Hidden Trespasses: The Price of Sexual Transgressions

Shepard focuses the play around the idea of a secret and horrific act (Dodge's murder of the illicit baby birthed by Halie), but Dodge's decision to kill the child rests solely on another hidden transgression, namely, the forbidden affair between Tilden and his mother. Indeed the hidden trespasses that the family attempts to obscure throughout the play all are related in some way to sexual transgressions. These transgressions affect the family dynamic in ways that are made explicit throughout their interactions. Dodge no longer trusts Halie around other men, and Tilden's "trouble" in New Mexico causes him to regress into an almost childlike state. The price of sexual trespasses causes psychic disconnections in more than just the central characters: Bradley attempts to usurp his now-dying father's power, while Vince becomes an unknown outsider to the family.

Shepard suggests early in the play that secret sexual transgressions exist for each member of the family. Dodge and Halie play a kind of game with each other in act 1 as she seems to joke about her sexual exploits with other men. Dodge pretends not to be affected, but his anger is palpable. Speaking about race tracks, Halie goads Dodge into a conversation:

HALIE'S VOICE: They used to race on New Year's! I remember that.
   . . . Before we were married they did! . . . I went once. With a man.
DODGE: Oh, a "man."
HALIE'S VOICE: What?
DODGE: Nothing!
HALIE'S VOICE: A wonderful man. A breeder. . . . He knew everything there was to know.
DODGE: I bet he taught you a thing or two huh? Gave you a good turn around the old stable! . . . When was this anyway?
HALIE'S VOICE: This was long before I knew you.
DODGE: Must've been. . . . And he never laid a finger on you I suppose?
   (65–66)

Dodge's question hangs in the air and remains unanswered, but Halie's silence affirms that she and her "escort" clearly had a sexual relationship. Though she insists that the affair happened before she was with Dodge, her half-hearted confession might suggest that this event happened during her marriage. Regardless, Halie's potential for sexual misconduct (and her ability to cover up her hidden sexual relationships) looms throughout the play.

As a result of Halie's hidden relationships, Dodge supposes that her relationship with Father Dewis is also an affair. When Vince asks where his grandmother is, Dodge responds, "Don't worry about her. She won't be back for days. She says she'll be back but she won't be. . . . There's life in the old girl yet" (87–88). Because of Halie's indiscretions, even Shelly feels the brunt of Dodge's misogyny. He tells Vince, "She could get me a bottle. She's the type a' girl that could be get me a bottle. Easy. She'd go down there. Slink up to the counter. They'd probably give her two bottles for the price of one.

She could do that" (94). Dodge conflates all women to the image he has of Halie: sexually promiscuous, unfaithful, and duplicitous.

When Father Dewis and Halie return in act 3, it appears that Dodge's suspicions might be confirmed. Both seem to be drunk and have spent the night together. After Dodge's confession, Dewis leads Halie upstairs to calm her down. No character ever explicitly states that Halie and Dewis are having an affair, but the suggestion of their relationship is enough to cause concern. Dodge's implication of Halie's incestuous affair suggests that Halie's relationship with Father Dewis might not be so innocent. At the end of the play, Father Dewis tells Vince about Halie, "She's going to need someone. I can't help her" (131), an implication by Shepard that Dewis has abdicated his position as Halie's lover. It is significant, then, that the "someone" to "help her" arrives in the form of a potential former lover (her son Tilden) carrying the bones of their dead child, a concrete consequence of their incestuous relationship.

Just as the relationship between Dewis and Halie is ambiguous, Shepard never fully explains what happened to Tilden in New Mexico that caused him to have to return to his family's home in Illinois. All we really understand of that time is Dodge's assertion that his son "had a little trouble back in New Mexico. That's why you came out here" (70), and Tilden's confession that he was "lonely" there (71). Dodge hints that Tilden's problems may have stemmed from a relationship: he asks Tilden, "Were you with somebody?" (78), but the young man only offers, "I was alone. I thought I was dead." While we do not know exactly what Tilden has done, we do know that Dodge does not trust him around young women. As he and Shelly talk, Dodge becomes increasingly irate—not simply over the fact that Tilden might confess—but what Tilden might do to her. "Tilden? You leave that girl alone" (103), he yells at his son. Underneath the confession, there is also an implicit threat of sexual violence that is later fulfilled by Dodge's son Bradley, who demands that Shelly open her mouth so that he may put his fingers inside of her. This pseudo-rape has the feel of a sexual violation, and Shelly equates it later with sexual assault: "You stuck your hand in my mouth and you call me a prostitute!" (120). As the secret sexual transgressions of the family are revealed, it becomes clear that Tilden and Halie's love affair is not the only taboo that they must try to obscure: each member of the family has a sexual secret to hide, one they will obscure at any cost.

Emotional Inheritances: Power and Masculinity

When Shelly and Vince first arrive at the house on their way to New Mexico, Shelly jokes with her boyfriend about how the house and its grounds exude the typically middle-class American image of family: "It's like a Norman Rockwell cover or something," she says of the house, "where's the milkman and the little dog. What's the little dog's name? Spot. Spot and Jane. Dick and Jane and Spot . . . and Mom and Dad and Junior and Sissy" (83). Upset by her teasing, Vince pleads with her to stop laughing, saying, "Come on! It's my heritage. What dya' expect?" (84). Heritage—especially the lessons passed down from father to son—become an especially important theme in *Buried Child,* with the cycle of secrecy and abuse that exists within the family occurring primarily because it is passed down endlessly from father to son. In the same way that Weston teaches an abhorrent masculinity to Wesley in *Curse of the Starving Class,* Dodge's emotional heritage leads to a legacy of violent, powerful masculinity that damages each of his sons.

The dynamic of Dodge as the "head of the household" also becomes an incredibly complicated idea in *Buried Child.* It is clear from the opening that the old man no longer represents the absolute head of masculine power in the house. He sits on the couch dying slowly, unable to stand or move without difficulty. Tilden's illicit love affair with his mother might be read as an attempt to wrest control of the family away from Dodge, but that action is ultimately defeated by the old man's drowning of the baby; the act cements his place as the head of the household. When Tilden returns from New Mexico, he is in no position to fight for control of the family: he is instead hollow and broken. In the absence of Dodge, Tilden, and the deceased Ansel, the power dynamic of the family clearly shifts to Bradley.

Bradley is an interesting character in *Buried Child.* Of all the men that appear onstage, the only person with fewer lines is Father Dewis. However, in his entrance in act 2, Bradley clearly exudes masculine power. Bradley belittles Dodge and Tilden in front of Shelly for his own amusement: "He used to be an All American. Quarterback or Fullback or somethin' . . . he used to be a big deal. . . . This one too. . . . You'd never think to look at him would ya'? All bony and wasted away" (105). Even from his first entrance, Bradley appears to be the bully of the family, the one who lords his masculine power over his family. When Shelly tells him to "shut up," his rage boils over: "HEY! MISSUS. Don't talk to me like that. Don't talk to me in that tone a' voice. There was a time when I had to take that tone a' voice from pretty near everyone. (*motioning to* DODGE) Him, for one! Him and that half brain that just ran outta' here. They don't talk to me like that now. Not any more. Everything's turned around now. Full circle. Isn't that funny?" (106). In his role as the only "whole" son, Bradley becomes the arbiter of what is right and wrong for the family. Bradley is especially interested in how the family appears to the outside world. Halie notes that he even "feels responsible" for

Dodge's "appearance" (68), and in one of the more darkly comic moments of the text, Bradley cuts Dodge's hair, reversing the roles of father and son. In the upside-down world of the family, Bradley becomes the father, the central masculine force keeping the family together. Act 1 ends with Bradley cutting his father's hair, and as act 2 opens, the man has been emasculated by his younger son. The stage directions note, "His hair is cut extremely short and in places the scalp is cut and bleeding" (83). In his role as the central masculine power, Bradley's presence is felt throughout the play, even before he enters. When Halie sees that Tilden has covered Dodge in corn husks, she scolds them both, "You better get this cleaned up before Bradley sees it. . . . Bradley's going to be very upset when he sees this. He doesn't like to see the house in disarray. He can't stand it when one thing is out of place. The slightest thing. You know how he gets" (76).

But the audience learns that Bradley is, like Tilden, a broken man; only, in this case, his affliction is both physical and mental: he is an amputee with a wooden leg. When he is awakened by his mother in act 3, Bradley appears to be no more than an overgrown child hollering, "Gimme that blanket! . . . That's my blanket!" (115). And, later in the act, when Shelly grabs his wooden leg, Shepard makes it clear that, without the prostheses, Bradley has absolutely no power. He whimpers childishly, "Mom! Mom! She's got my leg! She's taken my leg! I never did anything to her! She's stolen my leg!" (120). Without his leg, Bradley loses all of his power. He cannot stop Shelly from berating his mother, nor can he accost Dodge for his confession to Father Dewis. Though he frantically tries to keep his family together by screaming over Dodge's words, "Nothing ever happened that's bad! Everything is all right here! We're all good people!" (122), Bradley loses the battle. All he can offer is the pitiful, "If I had my leg you wouldn't be saying this. You'd never get away with it if I had my leg" (123).

Dodge's emotional inheritance seems to be a violent masculinity that is expressed by wielding absolute control over each member of the family. The lesson is compounded by Bradley in his guise as pseudo-tyrant, and Shepard explores how Vince learns the price of Dodge's inheritance in his return in act 3. Coming back drunk after being in town (a state that connects him to Dodge, who drinks for most of the play), Vince approaches the family house as though he were a soldier fighting a war. He smashes bottles against the porch, wrestles with Bradley, and finally receives the house in Dodge's spoken will. Though Shelly begs him to leave, Vince decides that his position as head of the household is his true destiny: "I've gotta carry on the line. I've gotta see to it that things keep rolling" (130). As he assumes control over the house and its belongings, Shepard notes that he "teases BRADLEY closer up left

corner of the stage . . . [and] throws BRADLEY's wooden leg far off stage left"
(131). Vincent and Bradley have traded roles, and it is Vince, not Bradley,
who eventually becomes the emotional heir to Dodge as well as the inheritor
of both the family's house and masculine power. Further confirming the idea
that Vince has taken his grandfather's place, the young man lies next to the
dead Dodge "in the same relationship" (131), his body position echoing the
old man's.

As Tilden slowly walks up the stairs with the body of his dead child in the
final moments of act 3, the play concludes with no real resolution. Though
the curse seems to have been lifted, the carousel of characters continues to
go round with no real shift away from the suffocating cycle of masculine
violence. Vince has assumed his grandfather's place; Bradley is once again
the simpering, younger child; Tilden moves toward a confrontation with his
mother and an acknowledgment of their sexual transgression. The damage of
sexual secrets, the abuse of masculine power, the curse of familial identities,
and the tenuousness of memory never resolve themselves. While *Buried Child*
does not offer a comprehensive answer to any of these problems, Shepard
does continue his exploration of the structure of the family and the difficulty
of articulating its authentic essence in his final entry in the family trilogy,
True West.

CHAPTER 5

The Authentic Family
True West

In the final play of what later came to be known as his family trilogy, Shepard pared down the number of central characters from six to just two. In *True West*, brothers Austin and Lee vie for control over their identity within the family, whether as protector of their father or the heir to his masculine authority over the family. Unlike in *Curse of the Starving Class* or *Buried Child*, however, in *True West*, each brother asserts, relinquishes, reestablishes, and cedes control over the course of the play. Because the central conflict of the play focuses on the relationship between the brothers, *True West* distills the epic power struggles among the families in Shepard's earlier plays into an examination of larger problems, including the heritage of the alcoholic father, the absent mother, and the fight to reclaim an identity from its inevitable conflation within the family. The action of the play might be compared to a game of chess in places; in other scenes, however, the game is more like a brutal dogfight. At the end the brothers hold their ground, and Shepard evokes the melodrama of a duel in a western movie. During these struggles for the upper hand, they fight over meaningless trophies like who gets the keys to the car, but they also wrestle over questions of honor, money, and power. By the end the childish contest becomes serious when they find themselves engaged in an epic clash with consequences they had not imagined.

While the setting recalls the realism of *Buried Child*, there is a certain sense of claustrophobia in *True West*. Shepard's notes describe his setting this way: "all nine scenes take place on the same set: a kitchen and adjoining alcove of an older home." Because escape and freedom from confinement are huge themes within *True West,* the fact that we witness the entire play within this small space underscores the frenzied nature of the two characters' interactions. They are caged like animals, and both have the same desire: to escape. The younger brother, Austin, never leaves the stage: the lights come up each scene with him trapped in the same place. Lee, the older, free-spirited brother, however, is allowed to enter and exit, but for the most part he, too, remains trapped. Other than one single moment, both brothers appear onstage together for the entirety of the play. Though they leave at various points during the action of the piece, those exits are done between scenes and away from the audience's perspective.

Shepard has made specific notes about the realism of *True West.* Appealing to future directors about the need for absolute realism, Shepard moved away from the dreamy and nonrepresentational aesthetic he employed in his early plays: "The set should be constructed realistically with no attempt to distort its dimensions, shapes, objects, or colors. No objects should be introduced which might draw special attention to themselves other than the props demanded by the script." One might read Shepard's adamant adherence to a nonstylized aesthetic in *True West* as a final break from the realm of Brechtian spectacle that he relied on in plays such as *The Tooth of Crime.* He further cautioned the directors that, "if a stylistic 'concept' is grafted onto the set design it will only serve to confuse the evolution of the characters' situation, which is the most important focus of the play."[1]

The two characters are clearly opposites, living binaries of the warring sides of the human psyche. As the younger brother, Austin is the button-downed suburban husband in his early thirties dressed in a "light blue sports shirt, light tan cardigan sweater, clean blue jeans, [and] white tennis shoes" (2). He possesses a quiet assurance of himself and his surroundings; as a writer, he lives a life of the mind. Unlike Lee, he has gone to college and studied, and now he is making a name for himself in the world of cinema in Southern California. His older brother, however, seems to be a drifter, a loner. Lee wears a "filthy white t-shirt, tattered brown overcoat covered with dust, dark blue baggy suit pants from the Salvation Army, . . . [with] two days' growth of beard, [and] bad teeth." He never went to college, he has had scrapes with the law, and he does not stay in one place for too long. Each piece of clothing is "exactly representative of who the characters are and [should] not [be] added onto for the sake of making a point to the audience" (4). Shepard's exploration of the dualism of character commences by simply putting these two foils together in the same space, and each dramatic moment begins from the conflict of their differing life experiences.

When the play opens on Austin and Lee, we learn that their mother has left town to visit Alaska. She asks Austin to watch her Southern California home while she is away; shortly after she leaves, however, Lee returns from a visit to their alcoholic father and decides to stay for a while with his brother. Within minutes of arriving in the suburban neighborhood, however, Lee gets antsy and takes Austin's car up into the foothills of the San Gabriel Mountains. Austin worries that Lee might try to burglarize the houses in his mother's peaceful neighborhood; he tries unsuccessfully to get his brother to leave the house while he writes. His fears are realized when—during a visit with a film producer (Saul Kimmer) about a screenplay he has written—Lee enters carrying a stolen television. Despite the awkwardness, Lee somehow persuades the producer to meet him for golf the next morning, when he promises to tell him a great movie idea, a western based on a true story. That night Lee persuades Austin to help write an outline for the western idea. Initially Austin is uninterested in the project, but when he senses that the screenplay might provide a springboard for his brother's disillusionment and eventual departure, he sets about to help him.

Act 2 begins after Lee and Saul have played golf. Lee boasts to Austin that he tricked the producer into buying his idea instead of Austin's by gambling on a single putt. Furious, Austin refuses to help Lee write the script and demands to meet with Saul. At the house Saul confirms that he did indeed agree to produce Lee's script over Austin's and encourages Austin to help write his brother's. Lee reveals that the money he gets from the script will go to their ailing and drunk father, news that enrages Austin even more. As night falls, the brothers switch personalities briefly as Lee bangs on the typewriter trying to get his script finished and Austin gets drunk. By the next morning, however, Lee has begun destroying the typewriter out of frustration over his inexperience with the written word, and Austin, in a misguided attempt to prove his bravery to Lee, has only managed to steal toasters from the houses in the neighborhood. Disgusted with their reversal, the brothers decide to escape. Austin begs Lee to take him with him into the desert, and Lee agrees on one condition: that Austin help him write the screenplay he had been trying to complete all night. Austin agrees.

The next morning, amid beer cans, a destroyed typewriter, and a wreck of a house, Austin and Lee's mother returns from Alaska while the boys continue to hash out a screenplay by hand. Upon his mother's arrival, Lee decides to make a quick exit back into the desert without Austin. Austin pleads with his older brother, who, unmoved, begins to raid his mother's antiques to pawn for money. In the midst of their argument, Austin takes the cord from the phone and wraps it around Lee's throat. Upset by their fight, their mother leaves to spend the night at a hotel. Stuck in a difficult position, Austin realizes he can neither kill Lee nor let him go. He tries to negotiate a truce with his older brother, but Lee passes out from lack of oxygen. Afraid he has killed him, Austin tries to leave, but as soon as he stands, Lee springs up and blocks the door. The lights dim on the two brothers circling each other menacingly, each waiting for the other one to make the first move. Like *Buried Child* and *Curse of the Starving Class*, *True West* ends without resolution. The brothers remain locked in an epic fight over their masculine power within the family, and there is no assurance that the fight will ever produce anything other than mindless destruction.

True West uses the two brothers to explore the notion of dualism, both in the characters of Austin and Lee, as well as the issues they raise throughout, such as those of authenticity and artifice, powerlessness and authority, and mind and body. While the subject is interesting as an exploration of the alternating consciousness in all of us, the trope of the "opposite" itself suggests that Austin and Lee are perhaps more emblematic of the shifting nature of dichotomies themselves and, specifically, of how opposites often intersect at key points of difference. Though Austin and Lee represent two distinct dramatic types, they change personalities throughout the play and, by the end, are far closer to each other than they were at the beginning.

Picking up the debate on familial power that he articulated best in *Buried Child*, both Austin and Lee constantly fight for control over their family. Though Lee is the older brother and, therefore, technically the one in charge, Austin has more control over his life. He owns a car, the brothers' only means of escape, and throughout the play the question of who controls the car mirrors the question of who has the upper hand in the relationship. Each brother struggles to win the respect of the other: Lee tries to write a screenplay as Austin does, and Austin breaks into his neighbors' houses to show Lee he is brave enough to steal from them. Neither endeavor really succeeds, however. As they fight to remain relevant to the each other, both brothers show how the power dynamic in the family is constantly up for grabs.

It should be noted, too, that *True West* is easily one of Shepard's funniest plays. While there are certainly comic elements in *Buried Child* and *Curse of the Starving Class*, *True West* sustains the humor throughout. Much of its humor derives from the darkly comic interactions between the brothers, but some of it is connected to the persistent and ever-mutating definition of authenticity that gets debated throughout the play. Lee tells Saul he has written a western, but unlike the hokey spaghetti westerns of popular culture, this one, he argues, is real, based on a true story. Likewise, Austin tries to sell his script of a romance based on the idea that it is beyond cliché, a real story dealing with real people in real circumstances. Behind all this is Shepard, who is attempting to say something authentic about the struggle of two brothers to remain relevant in their familial identities. The words "true," "authentic," "real," and "actual" are repeated and debated in the play until they are stripped of their meaning. By the end of the play, the audience understands that no one character—including Shepard himself—has ownership over authenticity. Shepard's title, *True West,* anticipates the futility of arguing over authenticity in relationship to philosophical ideas that are shared by many: brotherhood, honor, freedom, destiny, and escape.

Production History

Biographer Don Shewey has noted that, of all of Shepard's plays, *True West* was revised the most; Shepard completed almost thirteen drafts before he finished a version he felt was worthy of the stage.[2] Part of Shepard's anxiety was due to the play's relationship to his previous work, *Buried Child,* and its status as a Pulitzer Prize–winning masterpiece. The question of how to follow up such a successful production definitely weighed on Shepard, but much of the drafting of the play focused on stripping down the piece to its simplest dramatic moments. Robert Woodruff again helmed the play as it premiered at the Magic Theatre in San Francisco in July 1980, starring Peter Coyote and Jim Haynie. It had its first New York run at Joseph Papp's Public Theater in the fall of 1981, this time with the film actors Tommy Lee Jones and Peter Boyle. Though Woodruff began the New York run as director, he would quit during previews because of creative differences over the show's direction. Joseph Papp himself took over the role of director. Shepard blasted the production at the Public Theater before it even opened, largely because he felt the casting had been taken from Woodruff's hands and the director had been forced to work with actors who were marketable but not best for the parts. Partly because of Shepard's criticism—which the playwright offered despite never having seen either Jones or Boyle perform—critics seemed to delight in tearing apart the play's boring and tepid performances. The general assessment of the play was that it was the least successful of Shepard's major works to date.

What helped turn around critical opinions of *True West* was the 1982 revival by the acclaimed Chicago theater Steppenwolf, directed by Gary Sinise (who also played the part of Austin) and starring newcomer John Malkovich as a seething Lee. The production was such a hit that it was moved off-Broadway to the Cherry Lane Theatre, where it had a long run with many young actors (such as Randy and Dennis Quaid, Daniel Stern, and James Belushi) taking over for Sinise and Malkovich. It was during this run that critics began to appreciate the subtleties of the piece and how it distilled Shepard's complicated aesthetic down to intense dramatic moments between two people onstage. Critic Carol Rosen has noted that, of all of Shepard's plays, *True West* is perhaps most difficult to stage because "it can come across . . . as a somber *pas de deux* showdown between rival brothers," but she has added that the Steppenwolf production avoids those potential pitfalls by "tak[ing] a lighter approach . . . with an inspired silliness."[3] Whatever the reason, there remains little doubt that Sinise's Steppenwolf version established *True West*'s reputation as a worthy successor to Shepard's *Curse of the Starving Class* and *Buried Child*. Critics felt the play was a ponderous dud after the Public Theater's savage run, but Sinise reimagined the frenetic play as a bright character piece that satisfactorily concluded Shepard's meditation on the American family.

Personal and Professional Influences

As in his other plays, Shepard's explorations in *True West* owe a debt to Pirandello, Brecht, Beckett, and O'Neill, especially the (metadramatic/ postmodern) way the notions of character and authenticity are interrogated. Despite these heady concerns, *True West* does appear to be, on the surface, "his most straightforward play yet." Shepard's creation of Austin and Lee as a modern-day Cain and Abel, according to Shewey, reflects his past work "from the androgynes of *Cowboy Mouth* to the rock stars of *The Tooth of Crime* to the real blood relations in *Buried Child*,"[4] but the essence of the play becomes really just a supreme quest to understand "what it means to be a real man in today's world."

Shewey has also argued that "there's a lot about *True West* that is explicitly autobiographical," from Shepard's work as a screenwriter to his penchant for dressing and acting like Lee, the cowboy criminal and loner. The ghost of the father also haunts the brothers throughout the play, and much of what the audience learns about the "old man" is a distillation of Shepard's own experience with his father, including his old man's penchant for drinking, the story about the loss of his teeth, and his constant poverty. In the play, however, those stories become familial myths. It is important that the father has no physical presence on the stage, for he is a figure to be wondered at, to be imagined and revered solely through mythic narratives. The trajectory of the family trilogy seems to move toward emphasizing that story through the slowly disappearing patriarch. We see him throughout *Curse of the Starving Class*, though at the end of that play, his son and wife try to piece together his old stories to understand the dynamic he left them. In *Buried Child* we spend time with Dodge and learn his secret, after which, the old man dies onstage. But in *True West* the father is simultaneously absent and omnipresent: he informs every conversation, every power struggle between the brothers.

True West is also clearly interested in exploding another myth: the fantasy of the American West made popular by television and film. It presents Austin and Lee as characters who "have been catechized by the American belief in the open and efficacious frontier that promises renewal and rebirth."[5] But while the play does not exactly discredit the notion that the mythic land of the West offers possibilities for self-discovery, it does attack the neutered and suburban inhabitants who have denuded the land of any meaning. A central theme that recurs in *True West*—and throughout Shepard's entire family trilogy—is a continual dissatisfaction with progress in the form of housing developments and shopping centers. "No matter how far they drive on their desolate highways," J. Chris Westgate has claimed of Shepard's characters, "they cannot outdistance the ubiquitous signs of urbanization."[6] While Austin and Lee both long to escape to the mythic "true" West, the play ends with the acknowledgment that such a space no longer exists—and, perhaps, never did.

Shepard's setting and plot mirror the conventional action of the situation comedy and its dramatic precursor, Neil Simon's *The Odd Couple,* a play about two men trying to live together despite their clearly opposite personalities. The tone of the play appears light and comedic, and the humor that arises between the two brothers clearly references Simon's original work. However, Shepard has also looked to other dramatic artists for inspiration. Rosen has noted that the Austin-Lee conflict in the play is reminiscent of the "Teddy-Lenny battle in Pinter's *The Homecoming*,"[7] and the specters of Beckett's Hamm and Clov also appear in the interactions between the two brothers. With these disparate influences, one might conceivably call *True West* an existential comedy in which the humor comes from a dark understanding of the continually frustrating search for meaning and identity within one's own family.

Comedy and Humor

While *True West* is not the first play in which Shepard used humor, it might be the first to be considered a comedy. The conflict between the brothers creates outrageous situations that, at times, border on farce and parody, and the action of the play reminds the audience of a situation comedy on television, as both the brothers try to live together despite obvious differences. If Shepard channels Neil Simon's *The Odd Couple*, he makes Lee the obvious aggressor in the brothers' conversations. Austin engages Lee with polite, conversational questions that Lee disparages with sarcasm and bitterness. When Austin asks his brother if he'd like to sleep, for example, Lee calmly answers, "I don't sleep" (9).

There is also humor in Lee's perspective on the suburban world of his mother. He does not understand why she eats off antique plates, such as the one he finds with a decal of the state of Idaho: "Now who in the hell wants to eat offa' plate with the State of Idaho starin' ya' in the face. Every time ya' take a bite ya' get to see a little bit more . . . personally I don't wanna' be invaded by Idaho when I'm eatin'. When I'm eatin' I'm home" (10). Lee does not understand his mother's suburban middle-class world. He tries to fit in, but it is clear that he has no frame of reference. His idea of golf is something he has gleaned from popular culture. He does not really understand the game, though he does hustle Saul out of money on one putt. When he tries to persuade the producer to meet him for a round of golf, he counsels Austin on the finer points of the game: "We'll give ya' a quick run-down on the club faces. The irons, the woods. Show ya' a couple pointers on the basic swing. Might even let ya' hit the ball a couple times. . . . We'll have a little orange juice right afterwards. . . . Vitamin C! Nothin' like a shot a' orange juice after a round a' golf. Hot shower. Snappin' towels at each others' privates. Real sense a' fraternity" (17). Unsure of how to be authentic in a world that seems so artificial to him, Lee falls back on roles he has seen on television and in the movies. He does not understand the nuances of his brother's life, but he compensates by being overconfident; the disparity creates tension, which Shepard breaks through humor.

To everyone's surprise, Lee becomes a screenwriter overnight when he beats Saul on the final putt. However, he does not know how to work on the script; he does not understand the basics of how to write, type, or work for a set period of time. The silence of the house bothers him; all he can hear are the rhythmic sounds of the crickets. He tells his brother, "I'm a screenwriter now! I'm legitimate" (37), but he has no concept of what that job entails. He breaks the ribbon on the typewriter, and by scene 8, he is "smashing the typewriter methodically" with a golf club and "dropping pages of his script into a burning bowl set on the floor" (42). Lee finally gives up his illusion of living his brother's life and destroys the script for good.

Similarly Austin falters when he tries to play the role of a criminal. Toward the end of the play, desperate to prove himself to his brother, Austin bets that he can steal from his neighbors' houses. Although he succeeds in sneaking in, all he can force himself to steal from their houses are toasters.

Lee sneers at his crime, "What're you gonna' do with all those toasters? That's the dumbest thing I ever saw in all my life . . . and how many hundreds of dollars did you walk right past?" (43). But Austin revels in his actions, boasting, "There's gonna' be a general lack of toast in the neighborhood this morning. Many, many unhappy, bewildered breakfast faces. I guess it's best not to even think of the victims" (43).

Perhaps the most comic figure in the play, however, is the brothers' mother, who returns late in the final scene of the play. Like Ella and Halie, the mother in *True West* is a dim and disrespected member of the family. She initially returns home because she "started missing all my plants," but she finds, "Oh, they're all dead aren't they. You didn't get a chance to water I guess" (54). She explains excitedly to her sons that she has just learned of a Picasso exhibit at the museum. However, she reads the exhibit literally:

MOM: Somebody very important has come to town. I read it, coming down on the Greyhound.

LEE: Somebody very important?

MOM: See if you can guess. You'll never guess.

AUSTIN: Mom—we're trying to uh—

MOM: Picasso. Picasso's in town. Isn't that incredible? Right now.

AUSTIN: Picasso's dead, Mom.

MOM: No, he's not dead. He's visiting the museum. I read it on the bus. We have to go down there and see him. . . . This is the chance of a lifetime. Can you imagine? We could all go down and meet him. (54–55)

Austin cannot seem to convince his mother that it is Picasso's art and not the man himself that will be on display at the museum. Shepard's humor comes from the woman's unwillingness to relinquish her perspective, no matter how wrong it might be. Her personality immediately reminds the audience of both Lee and Austin and the fierceness with which each brother attempts to define himself as the truly authentic member of the family. But it is when both brothers step outside their roles that Shepard's humor accentuates what is one of his primary goals in *True West*: the exploration of duality.

Duality and Singularity

In an interview with Robert Coe, Shepard spoke of *True West* as, fundamentally, a play that explores the concept of man's dual nature: "I wanted to write a play about double nature, one that wouldn't be symbolic or metaphorical or any of that stuff. I just wanted to give a taste of what it feels like to be two-sided. It's a real thing, double nature."[8] With his references to Simon's *The Odd Couple* and a pseudo-sitcom setting, Shepard obviously sets up a binary of Austin/Lee to explore the notion of duality. From the very beginning Shepard has been at pains to show how Austin and Lee are the polar opposites of each other. Through a series of expository dialogues, we learn that Austin lives a life of the mind; as a writer, he invents worlds, characters, and dialogue for a living. He has been to college, studied at school, has a family and a stable life. Lee, on the other hand, is a drifter, a loner. He lives the physical existence of a rootless and homeless traveler. Unlike Austin, he has never been to college, does not have a family, and calls no one place home. Those differences are not the only clues we learn about the brothers' personalities: Austin is closer to his mother, while Lee constantly talks about his relationship with their father. When Austin confesses to his brother, "I love beginnings," Lee shoots back, "I've always been kinda' partial to endings myself" (48). Shepard has gone out of his way to present these two characters as diametrically opposed in every meaningful way. When the brothers are placed together side by side, conflict is inevitable.

Though he claims not to be interested in the "symbolic" or "metaphorical" narrative that such an exploration implies, Shepard is clearly examining the mind/body split in the guise of his two brothers. By the end of the play, Shepard has begun to interrogate the brothers' personalities and their supposed differences in order to expose their hidden connection to each other. During their interactions one cannot help but think about Shepard himself and how both characters display competing perceptions of the playwright himself: Austin, the stable and buttoned-down writer, who represents the acclaimed, Pulitzer Prize–winning public persona of Shepard; and Lee, the violent, renegade cowboy, who reminds audiences of the early Sam Shepard, the figure perpetuated through rock 'n' roll plays and his public love affair with Patti Smith. The brothers represent two sides of the same person, and neither version is more authentic. In fact both are completely artificial constructions that break down when pushed to extremes.

As a meditation on the author's dual public personas, one can read exchanges between the brothers as humorous metacritical perspectives on Shepard's maturation as a writer, as in this scene in act 1, when Austin attempts to explain his script to Lee:

LEE: You probably think that I'm not fully able to comprehend somethin' like that, huh?
AUSTIN: Like what?
LEE: That stuff yer doin'. That art. You know. Whatever you call it.
AUSTIN: It's just a little research.
LEE: You may not know it but I did a little art myself once.

AUSTIN: You did?

LEE: Yeah! I did some a' that. I fooled around with it. No future in it.

AUSTIN: What'd you do?

LEE: Never mind what I did! Just never mind about that. It was ahead of
   its time. (6)

Imagining the conversation between Lee and Austin as a dialogue between
the young, savage Shepard (author of plays such as *Cowboy Mouth* and
Operation Sidewinder) and the older, more mature Shepard proves to be
a useful interpretative technique for understanding *True West*. Just as Lee
makes "art" that he feels is experimental and "ahead of its time," so, too,
did the young playwright of *Cowboys* and *The Rock Garden*. If Lee is the
young, experimental Shepard, riddled with his personal demons of sex,
drugs, and excess, Austin is the professional writer, adored by critics and
held up as a model of contemporary American authorship. John Malkovich
notes as much when he says of the play, "People kept saying *True West* is so
commercial, but I think it's a more personal play than most of his. Shepard,
like Lee, defies all the things we're told we have to do to be successful. He
spent years in a loft picking his nose and writing really punk stuff with Patti
Smith, and then he wins a Pulitzer. He's like Austin when he shrugs off his
writing to go make all these movies, but then he'll turn around and, like,
trash Papp in *The New York Times*—that's such a Lee-like thing to do. Lee
is the side of Shepard that's always being strangled but never quite killed."[9]
Austin and Lee may represent the dichotomy of mind/body, but together,
they represent a singular vision of Shepard himself. Shepard's characters
suggest that opposites are nothing more than pieces that work toward a
collective consciousness.

   More than the notion of duality, the complicated multiple truths that
exist in supposedly simple, singular ideas interest Shepard. Though we are
invited to read Lee, on the surface, as a rough and confident cowboy, the man
clearly longs for a home. Wandering around the foothills of the San Gabriel
Mountains, Lee examines a house that affects him deeply: "Like a paradise.
Kinda' place that sorta' kills ya' inside. Warm yellow lights. Mexican tile
all around. Copper pots hangin' over the stove. Ya' know like they got in
the magazines. Blonde people movin' in and outta the rooms, talkin' to
each other. Kinda' places you wish you sorta' grew up in, ya' know" (12).
Despite the fact that the audience might reasonably expect that Lee abhors
such suburban boredom—indeed, Austin vocalizes that perspective when he
says, "I thought you hated that kind of stuff"—Lee exposes his complexity
by confessing his fantasy of wanting to live in a true home. Similarly, though

Austin has a family and a house, he longs to live the wild, untamed life of his brother: traveling from place to place without a clear home to settle in. When he gets drunk, Austin begs Lee to take him with him into the desert so that he can leave suburbia behind.

LEE: What're you, crazy or something? You went to college. Here you are down here, rollin' in bucks. Floatin' up and down in elevators. And you wanna' learn how to live on the desert!

AUSTIN: I do, Lee. I really do. There's nothin' down here for me. There never was. . . . There's nothin' real down here, Lee! Least of all me!

LEE: Well, I can't save you from that!

AUSTIN: You can let me come with you. . . .

LEE: Hey, do you actually think I chose to live out in the middle a' nowhere? Do ya'? Ya' think it's some kinda' philosophical decision I took or somethin'? I'm livin' out there 'cause I can't make it here! And yer bitchin' to me all about your success!

AUSTIN: I'd cash it all in a second. That's the truth. (49)

Austin's repressed suburban life has created a strong desire to break free from his family and live like an untamed animal. Throughout the play the image of the coyote—wild and vicious—and its connection with the domesticated dog—tame and submissive—is used to explain the two brothers. Lee represents the coyote (vicious, loud, territorial), and Austin represents the domesticated suburban dog. In Shepard's Darwinian world, the coyotes hunt the dogs, but they cannot attack them in the peaceful, suburban neighborhood. Austin explains, "This is the time of morning when the coyotes kill people's cocker spaniels. Did you hear them? That's what they were doing out there. Luring innocent pets away from their homes" (45). By the end of the play, however, Austin has become the aggressor, the alpha male. He strangles Lee to the ground, subduing him. The roles in the pack have changed, and Austin and Lee end the play having changed their roles as well. Though Shepard has created his brothers as easily definable types, he has also deflated his audience's expectations of who Lee and Austin really are by each brother's secret desire to live the other's life.

The expectations of the audience are further deflated by Lee's declaration that he has the film script of a "true" western movie inside of him. When Lee steps into his brother's terrain—the life of the mind—it causes all sorts of psychic disruptions that *True West* explores through disruptions in the setting. As Lee accidentally walks in on Austin's movie pitch, he excitedly tells the producer about his own idea for a movie. At first, Lee claims that script writing is not his talent, but he quickly convinces Saul that he has a good idea:

LEE: I got a Western that'd knock yer lights out.

SAUL: Oh really?

LEE: Yeah. Contemporary Western. Based on a true story. 'Course I'm not a writer like my brother here. I'm not a man of the pen.

SAUL: Well—

LEE: I mean I can tell ya' a story off the tongue but I can't put it down on paper. That don't make any difference though does it?

SAUL: No, not really.

LEE: I mean plenty a' guys have stories, don't they? True-life stories. Musta' been a lota' movies made from real life. . . . So ya' think there's room for a real Western these days? A true-to-life Western? (18–19)

Even though he claims not to be a "man of the pen," Lee is convinced that he has a good idea, and he enlists Austin to help him fashion an outline. Together the brothers argue over plot points and character choices as they create the skeleton of the idea that Lee presents to Saul during their golf adventure. Deep into their discussions, each brother recapitulates his desire to escape his own life and live as the other:

LEE: I always wondered what'd be like to be you.

AUSTIN: You did?

LEE: Yeah, sure. I used to picture you walkin' around some campus with yer arms fulla' books. Blondes chasin' after ya.'

AUSTIN: Blondes? That's funny.

LEE: What's funny about it?

AUSTIN: Because I always used to picture you somewhere.

LEE: Where'd you picture me?

AUSTIN: Oh, I don't know. Different places. Adventures. You were always on some adventure.

LEE: Yeah.

AUSTIN: And I used to say to myself, "Lee's got the right idea. He's out there in the world and here I am. What am I doing?" (26)

Shepard's presentation of both brothers as symbolic opposites proves disingenuous. Austin and Lee do not exist as such tidy, compartmentalized characters. Shortly after their conversation, the brothers do, indeed, attempt to live each other's life, but neither can totally sustain the effort. Lee cannot use a typewriter or work in the peaceful seclusion of their mother's suburban house, and while Austin attempts a life of crime, all he can steal are his neighbors' toasters.

As Lee tries to come up with his script, a drunk Austin offers an interpretive thought outside the action of the play: "Here's a thought. Saul Kimmer . . . he thinks we're the same person. He does! . . . Thinks we're one and the same" (36–37). In speaking outside of himself, Austin makes what might be Shepard's central point: that an exploration of plurality really opens up more spaces for connections than it articulates differences. Austin and Lee might represent two opposing aesthetics, but both philosophies are a part of a singular perspective rooted in a familial identity. When Lee replies that Austin's crazy drunk idea reminds him of "the old man," Austin replies, "Yeah, well, we all sound alike when we're sloshed. We just sorta' echo each other" (39). The differences of personality disappear when one considers the connection Austin and Lee have to their familial identity. What the brothers share that supersedes all of their petty differences of personality is a connection to their father and an inability—like Wesley, Vince, and Tilden—to escape their father's emotional inheritance.

Presenting the play through a metacritical, postmodern lens allows the notion of characters and their differences to be interrogated. In Lee's screenplay two central figures oppose each other; they remain engaged throughout the work in an epic struggle for power. Clearly Lee's idea mimics Shepard's trajectory in *True West;* thus Austin's criticism of Lee's creation of the central protagonists has a double meaning: "Those aren't characters. . . . Those are illusions of characters. . . . .Those are fantasies of a long lost boyhood" (40). Through his own illusory character, Shepard channels a key point of contention in his supposed exploration of duality: that it is not real; it cannot be articulated without artifice. The play ends up presenting its audience with the inescapable singularity of family—how one cannot escape the power struggles set up by the father and how the desire to leave the shady borders of the family ultimately leads to frustration.

The Keys to the Car: Power and Escape

One refrain that repeats throughout the play is a variation of the line "Give me the keys to the car." Unsure as to how Lee gets to his mother's house, the audience is nevertheless clear on one thing: Austin's car represents the only means of escape and freedom for either brother. Because the car belongs to Austin, Lee's attempts to "borrow" his brother's car can be read as attempts to wrest power from him. If Shepard's meditation on duality and singularity presented an opportunity to explore authorship, control over the car eventually comes to represent the same desire for authorial control over the story of the brothers' identities and their place within the family. Most every scene ends with one brother lording power over the other, and that brother usually always has the keys to Austin's car.

During the brothers' first exchange about the car, one understands that it represents more than just a vehicle. The stakes of their conversation get higher and higher until Lee explodes:

LEE: Now all I wanna' do is borrow yer car.

AUSTIN: No!

LEE: Just fer a day. One day.

AUSTIN: No!

LEE: I won't take it outside a twenty mile radius. I promise ya'. You can
  check the speedometer.

AUSTIN: You're not borrowing my car! That's all there is to it.

LEE: Then I'll just take the damn thing.

AUSTIN: Lee, look—I don't want any trouble, all right?

LEE: That's a dumb line. That's a dumb fuckin' line. You git paid fer
  dreamin' up a line like that?

AUSTIN: Look, I can give you some money if you need money.

LEE: Don't you say that to me! Don't you ever say that to me! You may be
  able to git away with that with the Old Man. Git him tanked up for a
  week! Buy him off with yer Hollywood blood money, but not me! I can
  git my own money my own way. Big money! (8–9)

What starts as a negotiation over the right to use his brother's car ends up as a violent confrontation over Lee's place in the family. He remains determined to prove that he is not like his father, a drunk, homeless charity case; rather he defines himself in much different terms, as an independent man who does not need help from anyone.

Eventually Austin relents and lets Lee borrow his car. When Lee returns, however, it is clear that he has stolen a television during his joy ride. Lee walks in with the stolen loot, interrupting Austin's business deal with Saul, and tries to get the producer to listen to his own pitch for a western movie, a transparent attempt to wrest control from his brother. As soon as Saul leaves, Austin demands the keys back from his brother, but instead of relinquishing control, Lee "doesn't move, just stares at AUSTIN, smiles" as the light fades onstage. Though Austin begins the early scenes in control of his story, Shepard signifies Lee's authorial takeover through his refusal to give back the keys to his brother's car. Later, as Lee begs Austin to help him with his outline, Austin first demands the return of his keys. Just as before, their dialogue about the car escalates to another near-violent confrontation:

AUSTIN: I'm not afraid of you either.
LEE: Then how come yer [helping me]?
AUSTIN: So I can get my keys back.
LEE: There. Now you got yer keys back. Go ahead. There's yer keys.
    Now what're you gonna' do? Kick me out?
AUSTIN: I'm not going to kick you out, Lee.
LEE: You couldn't kick me out, boy.
AUSTIN: I know.
LEE: So you can't even consider that one. (23)

Later in the scene Austin encourages Lee to write the screenplay and use the money from it to start his life over again. As he tries to build his brother up, he offers his mother's house and, in passing, the opportunity to borrow the car. At the end of the scene, Lee reminds him of his declaration: "Can I get the keys back before I forget? You said I could borrow the car if I wanted, right? Isn't that what you said?" (26). Begrudgingly Austin takes the keys out and puts them on the table as Lee "takes [them] slowly, plays with them in his hand." While the keys represent power and control, they also offer the potential for escape and freedom, two things that are core principles for Lee.

After demolishing Austin's typewriter in frustration, Lee decides it would be best to leave. He asks his brother how much gas he has in his car. Austin responds with sarcasm, "I haven't driven my car for days now. So I haven't had an opportunity to look at the gas gauge" (45). This subtle exchange reminds the audience both that Lee has been in control of the action for much of the play and that Austin still retains some power over his brother in that he owns the car. When Lee decides to leave the house at the end of the play, it is the thought of Lee's taking the car with him that incites Austin to attack his brother. As Lee packs up to leave, Austin rips the phone cord out of the wall and strangles him with it, yelling "You're not goin' anywhere! You're not takin' anything with you. You're not takin' my car! . . . Gimme back my keys, Lee! Take the keys out! Take 'em out!" (57). Eventually Austin wins the keys from his brother for the final time and, with them, seems to win the final struggle for power.

With his keys in hand, Austin negotiates a deal with his brother: "Let me get outa' here. Just let me get to my car . . . and I'll turn you loose" (59). It appears as though Austin has the upper hand in the brothers' final fight for control. However, just as he makes a move for the door, Lee jumps up, preventing Austin's escape. The final tableau represents a stalemate, an endgame in which neither brother has the upper hand. They end the play locked in deadly combat, like the tomcat and the eagle of *Curse of the Starving Class*. Though they are not yet engaged in the fight, they remain apart "keeping a distance between them ... still but watchful for the next move" (59), which recalls the final scene of *Buried Child* as Tilden approaches his mother's door. Both endings ask the audience to look beyond the final scene to the potential for a violent confrontation.

The Authentic Family

Like the two previous plays in his family trilogy, *True West* revolves around the actions (and sins) of the father of the family. However, unlike in *Curse of the Starving Class* and *Buried Child*, the father is not present onstage during the action of *True West*. Austin and Lee speak about "the old man" quite extensively, and the specter of the father hangs over the play. His absence creates his presence; because he is not onstage to offer his advice, Lee and Austin vie for control over his narrative voice. They discuss the ways their father would have handled situations, and embedded within that discussion, Shepard has inserted what might be the most critical question of the entire play: what is an authentic family? And as a corollary to that question, *True West* interrogates the very definition of authenticity itself.

It is no coincidence that Austin works in Hollywood (the land of illusions) or that he creates visions of an authentic world that supposedly invite audiences to suspend their disbelief. Because Shepard is engaged in the same work that Austin does in the play, the piece seems to address itself during key moments as Lee and Austin comment on the banality of dialogue, the flatness of characters, or the preposterousness of certain plot points in the script. Lee enters into the world of imagination skeptical of the power of art, but he also becomes seduced by its possibilities.

Lee comes to visit Austin from his father's place, and his connection with his father is clear from the first mention of "the old man." Lee notes that his father "told me about all you. . . . He told me. Don't worry" (7). When he gets the idea to sell his outline to Saul, Lee imagines the money could "get the old man outa' hock" (25), but Austin is not so sure that it is a good idea. "I gave him money," Austin says, "I already gave him money. You know that. He drank it all up!" (33). Still, Lee believes in the idea, and he wants to give his father a new life. Like Wesley in *Curse of the Starving Class*, he wants to offer his father a chance to start over again, and the money from selling his script offers him a way to do just that. The project that was once of personal significance to Austin—his idea of a romance with realistic characters—morphs into a project with personal significance to Lee: significantly the idea changes, from a romance to a western, and throughout the composition of the screenplay, Lee and Austin argue constantly over its authenticity.

From the very beginning Lee imagines his film as being based "on a true story . . . a real Western . . . a true-to-life Western" (19), but Austin objects to the way Lee creates his plot. "It's not like real life! It's not enough like real life," he argues, "Things don't happen like that" (21). In the middle of their argument, Lee suddenly threatens his brother over their dispute. Though Austin claims that their relationship as brothers should mean something, Lee argues that familial violence is the most authentic kind: "You go down to the L.A. Police Department there and ask them what kinda' people kill each other the most. What do you think they'd say? . . . Family people. Brothers. Brothers-in-law. Cousins. Real American-type people. They kill each other in the heat mostly. In the Smog-Alerts. In the Brush Fire Season. Right about this time a' year" (23–24). Gradually the struggle between the characters in the brothers' screenplay comes to represent the conflict between the brothers themselves in Shepard's world, and the Old West duel Lee imagines could easily connect with the power struggle between the brothers as they vie for authorship.

Lee is concerned with the reality of his characters and the world they inhabit, but he imagines his protagonist and antagonist as cardboard cutouts of western stereotypes: the good guy and the bad guy. He imagines each as, ultimately, powerless over the other one, constantly unsure of the power dynamic. At the end of act 2, he articulates their conflict, and one might imagine it as Shepard's own summary of the psychological struggle between Lee and Austin in *True West*: "So they take off after each other straight into an endless black prairie. The sun is just comin' down and they can feel the night on their backs. What they don't know is that each one of 'em is afraid, see. Each one separately thinks that he's the only one that's afraid. And they keep ridin' like that straight into the night. Not knowing. And the one who's chasin' doesn't know where the other one is takin' him. And the one who's being chased doesn't know where he's going" (27). Like the men in Lee's story, Austin and Lee have no clear idea who is in control of the story of their lives.

They both fight for power to tell their own story, but ultimately their actions reveal only their powerlessness. As Austin learns more about Lee's screenplay, he finds it lacks the very "ring of truth" (35) that Saul claims it has. The script, in fact, comes not from the recall of an authentic moment in Lee's memory but from the action taking place onstage before them. The story may not be the old, romantic idea of the West celebrated in the films of John Wayne, an idea that Austin correctly asserts is a "dead issue! It's dried up," but it follows the same ethos of the plot, world, and characters of the hackneyed western film.

Eventually the brothers come to the same conclusion that the audience does: that the story of their lives is more authentic and compelling than any prefabricated or generic narrative. Drunk with Lee, Austin tells the story of how his father lost his teeth: "Yeah, he lost his real teeth one at a time. Woke up every morning with another tooth lying on the mattress. Finally he decides he's gotta' get 'em all pulled out but he doesn't have any money. Middle of Arizona with no money and no insurance and every morning another tooth is lying on the mattress. . . . He begs the government. G.I. Bill or some damn thing. . . . And they send him out the money . . . but it's not enough money. . . . So he locates a Mexican dentist in Juarez who'll do the whole thing for a song. . . . Dentist takes all his money and all his teeth. . . . Then I go out to see him, see. I go out there and I take him out for a nice Chinese dinner. But he doesn't eat. . . . And then we go out to hit all the bars up and down the highway. . . . And in one a' those bars up and down the highway, he left that doggie bag with his teeth. . . . Now that's a true story. True to life" (42).

The story of their father's lost teeth may be the most compelling narrative of the play. Though it seems complicated and humorous, it also evokes a sense of their father's hopelessness, a condition Lee has inherited. And the story is all the more "true" because Shepard has based it on his own father, "although it was Shepard's sister Roxanne who took the old man out for the Chinese meal that cost him his teeth," according to Shewey.[10] Shepard suggests that the most authentic stories are those embedded within the family, and despite each brother's insistence that their idea for a screenplay is the truest example of real life, Lee and Austin become the authentic characters they themselves seek.

As he struggles to leave the house, Lee takes his mother's antique plates and cutlery, no doubt to pawn them down the road. When she asks him if he can borrow plastic cutlery instead, Lee explains, "It's not the same. Plastic's not the same at all. What I need is somethin' authentic. Somethin' to keep me in touch" (56). The disease of authenticity infects both brothers throughout the play. They rage to understand how to maintain a touchstone with reality in the face of their imagined existences.

Austin's world as a writer constantly has him inventing stories, characters, and worlds, and Lee has no connection with home. Each brother believes the other has a monopoly on the authentic, and they both claw, scratch, and fight to gain some control over the direction of their own lives, to finally have something to keep them "in touch" with who they are. Shepard ends the play with the brothers facing off in an epic duel, and it seems clear that the other brother is what grounds and keeps each brother connected to his reality: the world of the family.

CHAPTER 6

Chaos and Connection
The Later Works, 1983–2009

By the beginning of the 1980s, Shepard had become the most recognizable and prolific working American playwright of his generation. His plays had been produced throughout the country, and the completion of his family trilogy was heralded as one of the defining accomplishments of the American theater. Writing in the shadow of his own popularity, Shepard found it difficult to complete a new play. After his exploration of three-act family dramas, Shepard found that he could not write the one-act form as feverishly as he had in the 1960s. His next two plays borrowed heavily from the ideas he had explored in the family trilogy—dual nature, defining one's identity, the disintegration of familial bonds, and the violent competition for recognition within personal relationships. However, while his next two plays do not have the same investment with the family that *Curse of the Starving Class*, *Buried Child*, and *True West* share, they do investigate the consequences of violent familial competition. Both *Fool for Love* and *A Lie of the Mind* contain abusive family relationships. In *Fool for Love*, May and Eddie attack each other verbally, while in *A Lie of the Mind*, Jake beats his wife Beth until he believes he has killed her. The dark turn in Shepard's plays coincides with some personal darkness in his real life as well. At the time he was composing both plays, Shepard was experiencing a difficult breakup with his wife, O-Lan, and beginning a new relationship with film star Jessica Lange.

Fool for Love (1983)

Shepard's first play after *True West* clearly owes a debt to his exploration of double nature with the characters of Austin and Lee. However, in *Fool for*

Love, the characters are brother and sister—half-brother and half-sister, to be exact. The shift exposes Shepard's interest in exploring dual nature not just as an exercise to articulate competing versions of masculinity, but as a means of understanding the complicated way gender manifests itself as a central part of familial identity. Unlike his earlier plays, *Fool for Love* was difficult for him to write. Shepard found himself going through "about 16 versions of it, and every time I came back to the first five pages. . . . I've got literally at least a dozen different versions of the play. . . . They weren't just drafts. . . . I wrote twelve plays."[1]

The finished play takes place in a single act. Shepard explains before his stage directions that the "play is to be performed relentlessly without a break,"[2] and early on he establishes a chaotic, frenetic pace. Like the characters in the play, the audience is tasked with simply surviving the melee taking place onstage. When we meet the main couple for the first time, they are joined by an old man in a rocking chair, but he "exists only in the minds of MAY and EDDIE."[3] We learn later that the old man is actually the father of both May and Eddie, who are deeply in love with each other despite the knowledge of their shared parentage. It is clear from the beginning that their relationship is rocky: they argue heatedly in a shabby motel. He asks her to leave with him, but she refuses. Each time he tries to leave, however, she begs him to stay. When Eddie breaks down and agrees not to leave, May berates him and tells him she does not love him. In between these cycles of tenderness and rage, the old man alternately reminisces and prods Eddie to stand up for himself. Gradually we learn that Eddie has returned to May after leaving her for months—an abandonment that seems to happen every so often in their relationship—to be with a rich woman May has dubbed "the countess." While he has been away, May has begun to date Martin, a shy man who does lawn work around the town.

The countess arrives at the hotel and shoots out the back window of Eddie's truck. When she leaves, Martin enters to take May on their date to the movies and attacks Eddie, who he believes is trying to hurt May. As May freshens up for the date, Eddie tells Martin the story of their relationship: he explains that he and May began to date in high school before they knew they had the same father. The old man, who, up to this point, has been detached from the action in front of him, begins to take an interest in the story when May begins to narrate the final portion, including how her mother finds Eddie's mother. May explains how her mother tells Eddie's mother of the illicit relationship in hopes that she will forbid him from seeing May. Instead of stopping the romance, Eddie's mother shoots May's mother in the face. Distraught at this confession in front of a stranger, the old man demands that Eddie confirm the story, which he does. As Eddie and May embrace in the afterglow of the joint confession, the countess returns and destroys Eddie's truck. Eddie leaves to check on the wreckage, but May tells Martin that she knows Eddie has left her again. Sad and alone, she leaves the motel.

There are many echoes of Shepard's early plays in *Fool for Love*. The character of the old man clearly recalls Dodge as he sits decaying on the couch. Both men drink surreptitiously throughout the play, and both wear clothing that is literally falling apart at the seams (the jacket the old man wears has "stuffing coming out at the elbows"). Both also become involved in climactic confessions before a stranger in which they air their family secrets. Like Dodge in *Buried Child,* the old man cannot recognize his own flesh and blood. His denial of Eddie and May reminds the reader of Dodge's denial of Vince: "Amazing this is, neither one a' you look a bit familiar to me. Can't figure that one out. . . . Totally unrecognizable. You could be anybody's. Probably are."[4] There are also clear similarities between the old man and Shepard's own father. "One little talk, about Barbara Mandrell," according to Shepard, "is almost a verbatim conversation with my dad the last time I saw him. And there's a story about a cow field that he told my sister and she told me."[5]

May and Eddie recall Shepard's Austin and Lee and his Wesley and Emma, warring siblings who vie for their place in the family. During critical moments both Eddie and May act like children. It is clear that they have a relationship as lovers, but they exist simultaneously as childish siblings, a brother and sister engaged in repetitious, selfish arguments with each other over nothing. May threatens to kill Eddie's countess with a knife, and Eddie lies in wait for Martin in order to threaten him. To use May's terminology, each acts like "a jealous little snot-nosed kid"[6] toward the other. Shepard combines their relationship as brother and sister with their relationship as lovers in order to explicate the tragedy of the couple's situation: unable to live without each other as lovers, they are simultaneously unable to live together as siblings.

In previous plays Shepard articulated a dichotomy that he unpacked throughout the plays. In *Fool for Love,* Shepard uses duality itself as his central trope. Toward the end of the play, Eddie and the old man explain their tragic situation as the unraveling of a love that started out whole:

EDDIE: Our daddy fell in love twice. That's basically how it happened. Once with my mother and once with her mother.

THE OLD MAN: It was the same love. Just got split in two, that's all.[7]

Part of the exploration of the duality involves Shepard's exploration of the division between man and woman. As the man in the relationship, Eddie should have control over his own situation; he tries to manifest that control by constantly abandoning May. However, he cannot stay away. When May interrupts Eddie's story to offer the ending, the old man becomes irate at Eddie for refusing to take control over his own story. He screams at Eddie, "Stand up! Get on yer feet now goddammit. I wanna' hear the male side a' this thing. You gotta' represent me now. Speak on my behalf. There's no one to speak for me now! Stand up!"[8] To the old man, Eddie's refusal to stop May suggests an abandonment of his masculine power. Eddie and May should be kept apart, he imagines, because such a union would destroy him entirely. He begs Eddie to leave her alone: "Keep away from her! You two can't come together!"[9] For the old man, Eddie's love of his sister represents an unnatural desire, one that the old man reads as Eddie's failure to achieve his potential of authentic masculinity.

Shepard also explores the split between truth and fantasy. It is important that Eddie is a stunt man: he is not really a cowboy, he just plays at the role. Like Shepard's, his craft involves illusion and subterfuge. Shepard uses Eddie the same way he uses Austin in *True West:* to comment on the business of invention and storytelling. Eddie participates in stories that he knows to be false, but through the crafting of the lie, he is able to produce a truth. The old man exists onstage as an example of the paradox of imagination: he is clearly a shared figment of Eddie and May's imagination, and yet he speaks realistically to both characters. It is fitting then that early on in the play, the old man makes a crucial point about the truth of imagination:

THE OLD MAN: I thought you were supposed to be a fantasist, right? Isn't that basically the deal with you? You dream things up. Isn't that true?

EDDIE: I don't know.

THE OLD MAN: You don't know. Well, if you don't know I don't know who the hell else does. I wanna' show you somethin'. Something' real, okay? Somethin' actual.

EDDIE: Sure.

THE OLD MAN: Take a look at that picture on the wall over there. . . . Ya' know who that is? . . . Barbara Mandrell. That's who that is. . . . Would you believe me if I told ya' I was married to her?

EDDIE: No.

THE OLD MAN: Well, see, now that's the difference right there. That's realism. I am actually married to Barbara Mandrell in my mind. (27)

The point the old man makes is that imagination offers a glimpse into a personal truth. That the Barbara Mandrell speech came almost verbatim from Shepard's own father further speaks to the division between fantasy and truth, with Shepard mining the contents of his own life for his imaginative play.

Right after the old man's lesson on the truth inherent in fantasy, May confesses that her imagination has also infected her ability to know what is true. She tells Eddie, "I can't even see you now. All I see is a picture of you. You and her. I don't even know if the picture's real anymore. I don't even care. It's a made-up picture. It invades my head. The two of you. And this picture stings even more than if I'd actually seen you with her. It cuts me. It cuts me so deep I'll never get over it. And I can't get rid of this picture either. It just comes. Uninvited. Kinda' like a little torture."[10] Like the old man's picture of Barbara Mandrell, May's imagined picture of Eddie and the countess creates a separate reality that is perhaps more compelling than the truth. In the end *Fool for Love* becomes less a commentary on gendered binaries and more a meditation on the insidiousness of invented narratives. The joint story that Eddie and May tell to a hapless Martin may be complete fiction, but because they believe in its truth, the narrative exists just as surely as the old man does: as complete fact. The play ends with the old man reaffirming his belief in his imagined fantasy: "Ya' see that picture over there? Ya' see that? Ya' know who that is? That's the woman of my dreams. That's who that is. And she's mine. She's all mine. Forever."[11] Through his characters, Shepard also comments on the craft of playwriting and how its invented realities sometimes are more compelling and truthful than the "real world." It would be a theme he picks up again: an exploration of duality, especially its connection to invented worlds and gender trouble, appears in his next major, solo play, *A Lie of the Mind*.

A Lie of the Mind (1985)

A Lie of the Mind represents the cumulation of Shepard's reflections on double nature. *True West* begins this exploration with the investigation of familial identity and competing masculinities; *Fool for Love* expands it by emphasizing the role of separateness and coupling. *A Lie of the Mind* begins where *Fool for Love* ends—with the same unstable, violent relationship between an uber-masculine protagonist and his rattled but determined wife. While Shepard most certainly mined biographical elements for the play (Shewey finds his father's car accident, Shepard's relationship with Lange, and his friend Joseph Chaikin's stroke referenced in different moments in the play), the connections are not as direct as in his family trilogy. Here Shepard's personal connections serve as a beginning point for his characters, an anchor that grounds the playwright in key moments.

As in many of Shepard's pieces, the emotional inheritance from the father weighs heavily on all the characters in *A Lie of the Mind*. Just as Shepard used a conversation with his father about Barbara Mandrell in *Fool for Love*, he uses a moment from his father's funeral as the crux of *A Lie of the Mind*: "I had my dad cremated, you know? There wasn't much left of him to begin with. They give you this box with the ashes in it. The box is like it's got a spotlight on it or something, because that's *him*, and yet it's just this little leather box. . . . Two objects are the centerpieces of the service, the box and a little folded-up flag. I kept staring at the box the whole time I was reading . . . and I wondered if I was supposed to take the box or . . . I walked over and I picked up the box and I was . . . it was so heavy. You wouldn't think that the ashes of a man would be that heavy."[12] In a crucial moment during *A Lie of the Mind*, the main character, Jake, berates his mother about the location of his father's ashes. "Where's that box," he asks her of his father's remains, and when she retrieves it for him from under the bed, she also hands him "the flag they gave you at the service."[13] When Jake picks up the box, he notes, "This is him. . . . He's kinda heavy."[14] Like Shepard's father, Jake's father was in the service. Lorraine tells him that "we chased your daddy from one air base to the next. Always tryin' to catch up with the next 'Secret Mission.' Some secret."[15] And, like Shepard's father, Jake's father did not die a hero's death but was hit by a car. "He was no hero," Lorraine tells him, "Got hit by a truck. Drunk as a snake out in the middle of the highway. Truck blew up and he went with it."[16] Like Dodge, Weston, and the old man, Jake's father figures prominently in his son's perspective on his identity. The first act ends with Jake's blowing gently on the ashes and sending them into a plume of light onstage; the symbolic gesture suggests the process of letting go, a process Jake follows through on in the next two acts.

A Lie of the Mind takes place in three acts and is one of Shepard's last full-length plays. The play begins in the middle of a desperate situation: on the phone with his brother Frankie, Jake confesses that he believes has beaten his actress-wife (Beth) to death because of his paranoia over how she dressed when she left for her rehearsals. The scenes shift cinematically between Jake and Frankie trying to figure out what to do next and Beth recuperating in the hospital with her brother Mike. Though she has not died from her injuries, Beth is severely injured, and it is possible she has suffered brain damage. Lorraine (Jake's mother) and Sally (his sister) intervene and try to get Jake to come out of his depressive funk in the same way Mike tries to get Beth to walk and talk again. Lorraine persuades Jake to come home and live responsibility-free in his old boyhood room, while Meg and Baylor (Beth's parents) take her to their home.

While deer hunting back home, Baylor accidentally shoots Frankie in the leg. The man had come to plead mercy for his brother and to ask forgiveness of the family. While Mike is reticent to accept Frankie's apology, Baylor, Meg, and Beth welcome him. Beth remembers something about Frankie (possibly his voice), and the new memories spark a desire in her. She begins a clumsy flirtation with him that expands into full-blown crush. Meanwhile Jake escapes Lorraine's house with the aid of Sally and travels to Beth's parent's house, where he is caught like a dog by Mike. When he comes into the house humbled and humiliated by Beth's brother, he finds that Frankie and Beth have begun a strange romantic relationship. Rather than acting out viciously, he gives the two his blessing and, after declaring his undying love for Beth, retreats into the darkness. At the end of the play, as Sally and Lorraine torch their family home, Meg stands at the window in her house that overlooks a snowy field. Somehow she sees—across time and space—the fire burning down Jake's ancestral home and comments on how strange it is to see "a fire in the snow."[17]

Just as in *Fool for Love*, Shepard plays with duality—not simply the role of opposites with regard to his characters but also the physical binary of stage left and right. Shepard bifurcates the stage to emphasize each family's isolation. In the very first scene, Jake speaks to Frankie on a pay phone. The actors are onstage together, but Shepard makes it clear that they should appear miles apart. He notes that there should be the "impression of huge dark space and distance between the two characters with each one isolated in his own pool of light."[18] The sense of "shared isolation" continues as Beth and Mike's scenes are played out downstage left and Jake, Mike, and Sally's scenes are played on a stage-right platform. At the end of act 1, these separate worlds coexist in light as Jake sees a vision of Beth upstage left. Her hospital bed has been made up in "blue satin sheets. . . . She is simply his vision."[19] However, when Jake makes a move toward her, "the light on her blacks out. She disappears."

Similarly the two houses appear on different sides of the stage. The action that takes place in Beth's family's house happens stage left, while Jake's family stays stage right. However, in the middle of act 3, scene 3, the worlds begin to collide. Lorraine and Sally decide to burn down their house and run away. Together they light a match and ignite some papers in a nearby bucket. Shepard's stage directions note, "The fire in the bucket keeps glowing. Simultaneously, lights are rising center stage," as Jake enters Beth's world for the first time in the play. With Jake's entrance into Beth's family's house, there is a literal and figurative connection between the family's two worlds. The fire in the bucket continues burning throughout the final scene, and the play ends with Meg's metatheatrical comment on the fire at Jake's house: "Looks like a fire in the snow. How could that be?"[20] The line references the physical binary Shepard had set up throughout the play and its eventual conflation. Meg's ability to see the fire finally interrupts the isolation and separation between the families that Shepard had emphasized from the beginning of his play. Not only do the sides of the stage no longer represent two distinct worlds, but Meg's ability to see through the walls of time and space manifests the breakdown of the naturalism/expressionism binary that Shepard had asserted through his realistic presentation of the first two acts.

Shepard's bifurcation of the stage also suggests the duality of man/woman and of Jake/Beth. One gets a sense that Shepard has emphasized the dual roles because of their vitality: women need men, Beth needs Jake. In an interview with Jonathan Cott, Shepard explained his inspiration for the play came from "the incredible schism between a man and a woman in which something is broken in a way that almost kills the thing that was causing them to be together. The devastating break—that was the lightning bolt."[21] Characters in the play comment on the difficulty of maintaining relationships between men and women, but nowhere in the play does anyone suggest that existence is possible without a mate. Even as Baylor and Meg argue over the gendered perspective in one key moment in the play, Meg acknowledges the desperate need women have for their men:

MEG: Maybe it really is true that we're so different that we'll never be able to get certain things across to each other. Like mother used to say.

BAYLOR: Your mother.

MEG: "Two opposite animals."

BAYLOR: Your mother was a basket case.

MEG: She was a female.

BAYLOR: Meg, do you ever think about the things you say or do you just say 'em?

MEG: She was pure female. There wasn't any trace of male in her. Like Beth—Beth's got male in her. I can see that.

BAYLOR: I'm her father.

MEG: No. She's got male in her.

BAYLOR: I'm male! I'm her father and I'm a male! Now if you can't make sense, just don't speak. Okay? Just rub my feet and don't speak. . . .

MEG: I know what it is. . . . The female—the female one needs—the other.

BAYLOR: What other?

MEG: The male. The male one. . . . But the male one—doesn't really need
the other. Not the same way. . . . The male one goes off by himself.
Leaves. He needs something else. But he doesn't know what it is. He
doesn't really know what he needs. So he ends up dead. By himself.[22]

Despite the difficulty of communication—of sharing a perspective—Meg
argues that men and women, in their purest forms, have a physical need
for each other. She also claims, somewhat unconvincingly, that men do not
"really need" women in the same way. Her reading might have a kernel
of truth in it for Jake and Beth, but it does not explain the other complicated relationships in the play, such as the ones between Frankie and Beth or
between Meg and Baylor. Although Meg and Baylor seem distant and separate, they share a silent and meaningful kiss at the end of the play, proof of
their mutual need for each other. Baylor might argue that he would be better
off alone in a hunting shack, but he needs the restorative physical touch of
Meg to calm him down. In the end the only conclusion one can draw from
Shepard's insistence on emphasizing the separateness of men and women is
that the two are locked into a desperate and undying union based on their
mutual need for each other. While they might be forced apart for a while,
they cannot escape their addictive need for each other.

Shepard's exploration on the duality inherent in masculinity in *True
West* gives way to an examination of the duality of gender itself in *A Lie of
the Mind* and *Fool for Love*. In many ways *A Life of the Mind* is a satisfying conclusion to the exploration of dual nature in general as the relationship between opposites compels not because of difference but because of
similarity. Perhaps because the play seems so final, so conclusive, it is no
coincidence that it represents a major break in the author's artistic life. Asked
by an interviewer in 1987 about critics who said *A Lie of the Mind* left him
nowhere to go, the author responded,

> You can't pay any attention to that, because you've got other things to
> do. Being surrounded by parasitic people who feed off your work—well
> I guess you've just got to accept it. And I suppose some parasites are
> okay, because they take things off of you. Once, in New Mexico, I
> observed these incredibly beautiful red-tailed hawks—with awing span
> of five feet—which started out gliding in these arroyos way down low.
> And these crows come and bother them—they're after fleas and peck at
> the hawks and drive them nuts, because they're looking for something
> else. And I watched a crow diving at and bothering this one hawk, which
> just flew higher and higher until it was so far up that the crow couldn't

follow it anymore and had to come back down . . . [so the answer is to] outfly them. Avoid situations that are going to take pieces of you. And hide out.[23]

Shepard did, indeed, hide out. He would not write another play for six years, and when he returned, it would be with a piece that was not interested so much in deconstructing binaries but, rather, hearkened back to the experimental aesthetic he honed in the 1960s.

Shepard in the 1990s: Rebirth or Decline?

When *States of Shock* premiered in 1991, critics and audiences were eager to see what Shepard would make of his long break from writing. They anticipated his deft, critical eye dissecting both the encroaching anxiety about the dawning of a new millennium and the new excesses of American popular culture. But rather than inventing a new aesthetic, Shepard returned to the form, structure, characters, and action of his early plays. In *States of Shock*, *Simpatico*, and *Eyes for Consuela*, critics did not find the raw, unique voice of the countercultural radical; they found, instead, a playwright who had lost his voice. In his review of *Simpatico* in *Daily Variety*, critic Jeremy Gerard wrote of how "disheartening [it was] to watch this writer spin further and further out of the dramatic center,"[24] and even those critics who argued for merit in the three 1990s plays had to admit they were "by and large . . . failed attempts."[25]

States of Shock recalls Shepard's early one-act plays in several ways: the dialogue is often difficult to follow, characters do strange things for no apparent reason, and the staging of the action is much more expressionistic than realistic. Unlike his early plays, *States of Shock* was inspired not by an event from Shepard's life but by the media's coverage of the Gulf War of the early 1990s. Shepard found himself "outraged by the whole hoax" of the war, "the way everything is choked down and censored in the media."[26] But instead of turning the public against the war, the play had failed to make a connection. Shepard admitted, "I don't know what happened. It only succeeded in pissing off the critics, it seems like. That was part of its purpose. I don't know." Perhaps critics responded to what they saw as Shepard's stepping back into his past instead of moving forward. Regardless, *States of Shock* does have more in common with plays such as *4-H Club* and *Icarus's Mother* than it does with *A Lie of the Mind* or *Fool for Love*.

The play takes place in a diner, signified by a bare stage with a cyclorama, café chairs, and a red Naugahyde booth. The main characters are the Colonel, who is described as a "repulsive, military, fascist," and Stubbs, a wounded war veteran who spends most of his time in a wheelchair. They have come to the diner to celebrate the anniversary of the Colonel's son's death and Stubbs's strange connection to the event (apparently the bullet went through Stubbs's body and into that of the Colonel's son; the boy was killed instantly). Their solemn meal is interrupted by chaotic back-and-forth shouting matches in which Stubbs raises his shirt repeatedly to show his wound, barks at the couple across from them about his impotence, attempts to help the colonel piece together the events surrounding his son's death with toy soldiers, and is beaten by the Colonel for his insolence. The play ends with the revelation that Stubbs is, indeed, the Colonel's son, disowned by the man after he discovered his injuries. While the revelation is never affirmed by the Colonel, the suggestion seems to change the meaning of the play in its last few minutes. Rather than being an exploration of the machinations of America's war machine, it moves the piece into the familiar territory of father-son conflict.

While *States of Shock* dabbles in stereotype and pastiche—the Colonel wears relics of different time periods, including a Civil War saber, and the waitress is named Glory Bee—it also offers connections to several typical Shepard themes, including the fashioning of authenticity, the desire to escape crippling family relationships, and the undeniable connection between violence and sexuality. It is the latter theme that might be most prominent in the play. When the Colonel forces Stubbs to show the waitress his wound by lifting his shirt and exposing his chest, the veteran also divulges the pain of his sexual wound: "When I was hit I could no longer get my 'thing' up. It just hangs there now. Like dead meat. Like road kill."[27] His cry, "MY THING HANGS LIKE DEAD MEAT!!!" is repeated throughout the play to the waitress, the Colonel, and the couple sitting across from them. Stubbs begs the Colonel to take him back, to remember him, and he offers the possibility of regaining his phallic power as a means of becoming whole again. He asks him, "If my 'thing' comes back. If it grows straight and strong and tall—Will you take me back?"[28]

Just as in *Buried Child*, Shepard connects power with memory. Eventually Stubbs connects his impotence with the inability to remember. When he embraces Glory Bee in an odd moment, he begins to remember, an action that, strangely, cures his impotence. "My thing is coming back. . . . My thing is arising! I can feel it. . . . It's coming back! It's all coming back to me now!"[29] he tells the Colonel. He "remembers" how the Colonel, his father, changed his name, disowned him. He remembers how he was forgotten by his family, and he is able to finally confront the man with the truth. "YOU INVENTED MY DEATH," he screams.[30] Just as it takes disconnection and wounding to create Stubbs's impotence and amnesia, all it takes is a moment of connection with Glory Bee to heal his memory and restore his masculinity. By remembering who he is, Stubbs regains a sense of his masculinity and is able to take a position of power over his father, the domineering Colonel.

While the action between Stubbs and the Colonel takes place, a dark vaudeville act is played out one table over between an emasculating woman and a henpecked man. The couple waits throughout the play for chowder that never seems to come; all the while, the woman barks about how she'd like to speak to the manager. The man, however, says little. When the chowder arrives, he politely tells the waitress that he no longer wants it; she responds by dumping the bowl in his lap. As he tries to clean himself off with a napkin, the stage directions note, "THE WHITE MAN's cleaning of his lap slowly turns into masturbation."[31] The two scenes interconnect: as the Colonel barks at Stubbs to clean up his spilled food, Stubbs shoots back, "BECOME A MAN"[32] over and over while the man at the other table carries himself "to the verge of orgasm." The connection between the two moments are clear: both the White Man and Stubbs must assert their masculinity through their sexual power, and only when they achieve some kind of sexual freedom can they understand the scope of their masculinity.

Shepard's obsession over difficulties in asserting masculine power continues in his next two plays, *Simpatico* (1994) and *Eyes for Consuela* (1998). *Simpatico* is a much more straightforward play than *States of Shock*, and it has little of the experimental aesthetic that marked Shepard's work in the 1960s. The plot follows the business of horse racing and crime; the protagonists, Vinnie and Carter, long ago (and with the help of Vinnie's wife, Rosie) lured a high-ranking racing official into an affair and blackmailed him with photographic proof. When the play begins, we learn that Vinnie lives in squalor in California while Carter has become a wealthy businessman in Kentucky. Vinnie decides to come clean to the racing official they blackmailed (who is, like Vinnie, now paid by Carter to keep his mouth shut) and to take revenge on Carter (who has since married Rosie, the love of his life). His attempts to betray Carter and own up to his guilt in the matter fail, and he returns to his home to find Carter racked with anxiety and drunk. Satisfied his revenge is complete, Vinnie kicks him out of his house.

Simpatico investigates ways in which men can express their power over other men and how that power often wounds both parties. Leslie Wade calls the plot "one of Shepard's most utilized dramatic devices . . . setting two male characters in opposition and precipitating a reversal."[33] While the play traffics in devices and themes familiar to Shepard—the inescapable past, the desire to assert one's identity, and the shifting power dynamic between men—the end result feels recycled and stale. One review notes that the play appears to be "a B-movie script by someone who's read a lot of Shepard."[34] *Simpatico* lacked the complicated connections that Shepard's earlier plays forged between identity and gender, or family, or country.

Eyes for Consuela (1998), on the other hand, is a much more expressionistic play, one that operates, on some levels, almost as a parable. It also represented the first solo play Shepard had ever done that was based on an existing work; in this case Octavio Paz's short story "The Blue Bouquet" was the inspiration for the piece. Like *La Turista*, the play follows an American on vacation in Mexico, but unlike the urban landscape outside the hotel room in *La Turista*, the deep Mexican wilderness serves as the setting for *Eyes for Consuela*. The man, Henry, has come to Mexico to escape the recent mess his life has become: his wife has left him, and he has refused to follow her to Michigan. His career is also at a crossroads. In the midst of his soul searching, he is attacked by a local villager, Amado, who holds him captive in his own room while tormenting him by threatening to slice his eyes out as a trophy for his lover, Consuela. After pleading with Amado, Henry finds Consuela, who might or might not be an apparition, and she spares his eyes. Changed by his time with Amado and Consuela, Henry gives up the family heirlooms he has been traveling with and goes back to America and, one assumes, his wife. The play feels like a redemptive parable in which Henry, the arrogant and thoughtless capitalist American, comes to the impoverished Mexican jungle in order to find himself. Instead he is tested by the conditions that surround him and is forced, in the end, to realize his need for interdependence.

Eyes has connections to many Shepard plays—*La Turista, A Lie of the Mind, Seduced*, as well as others—but Wade notes that its ending, with Henry going back to live with his wife, might be the first play in which the central male does not allow himself "to be consumed by [his] compulsion" but makes an effort to move "towards the female's space."[35] The movement represents a fundamental shift for Shepard, away from the cynical destructive behavior of a typical Shepard male and into a more hopeful exploration of connection and dependence. However, while the play offered new possibilities, it still fared poorly with the critics, who once again felt it did not express anything visionary or new. Indeed the conclusion of many was that Shepard's moment had passed. His plays, which once contained vicious indictments of the excesses of masculinity, no longer connected with the culture of the 1990s but felt dated and old. Critics concluded that Shepard was not so much evolving as he was recycling. For scholars, however, Shepard's plays of the 1990s offered both connections with old preoccupations and themes as well as the potential for new explorations. While *States of Shock* or *Eyes for Consuela* lacked the complexity and multivocal commentary that plays such as *Buried Child* and *A Lie of the Mind* had, they did offer a unique voice that was, after almost thirty years, distinctly Shepard's.

Sam Shepard beyond the Millennium

Since 1998 Shepard has written four major plays: *The Late Henry Moss* (2000), *The God of Hell* (2005), *Kicking a Dead Horse* (2007), and *Ages of the Moon* (2009). While these plays are not as ambitious as Shepard's family trilogy, they do represent an evolution from his plays of the 1990s, in which the author has reverted to the familiar emotional territory of his early work. Starting with *The Late Henry Moss*, Shepard signaled a final return to the American family and his explorations of competing masculinities among brothers, sons, and fathers. *Henry Moss* also reconfigures the notions of time and space onstage as portions of the action take place in present time, while a good deal of acts 2 and 3 take place simultaneously in the past and present.

The play revolves around the figure of Henry Moss, who lies dead at the opening of the play. His sons, Earl and Ray, have come to pay their final respects to their father, but their grieving takes an immediate backseat to accusations and mistrust. Earl, the older, accuses Ray of shifting the anger over their father onto him, while Ray berates Earl for leaving him and their mother to suffer their father's abuse. While Earl is interested in making peace with his father, Ray is more interested in the circumstances of his death. He calls the taxi driver who last saw his father and asks him to recount the final moments of the old man's life. The taxi driver inadvertently reveals that Earl returned to confront Henry just before his death. Armed with this information, Ray torments a drunken Earl when he returns to his father's house early the next morning. He hits, kicks, and slaps his brother, and eventually forces him to scrub the floor. During the final moments of the play, the action shifts back to Henry's final night with Earl, where the father confesses to his son his terror at himself as he attacked Earl's mother on the night he decided to run away from his family. After his confession Henry lies down next to his new lover (and secret tormentor) and dies. The play ends with the brothers speaking the same inane dialogue that started the play, suggesting the circularity of the events and the slippery nature of remembering.

The Late Henry Moss feels like a conclusion to Shepard's lifelong obsession with his father. In an interview in 2000, Shepard commented, "The play concerns another predicament between brothers and fathers and it's mainly the same material I've been working over for thirty years or something but for me it never gets old, although it may for some audiences. This one in particular deals with the father, who is dead in the play and comes back, who's revisiting the past. He's a ghost—which has always fascinated me . . . the corpse is present in the play and the corpse comes alive. I don't know, I find that fascinating."[36] Like the specter of Shepard's own father that haunts his work, Henry Moss literally haunts the stage during the entirety of *The Late Henry Moss*. One critic has noted that the Moss family and the Shepards share many similarities—"the alcoholism, the shattering of doors and windows, the violence against wives and the attendant emotional injuries exacted upon the children, the move from Illinois to New Mexico . . . the ignoble deaths of fathers, and so on."[37] And yet, unlike the fathers of *Fool for Love, Curse of the Starving Class*, or *Buried Child*, Henry Moss comes to an epiphany before he expires: he realizes that he alone is culpable for the disintegration of his family and for the damaged and brutalized lives of his sons and wife. Remembering the night he beat his wife almost to death, Henry—just before he passes away—recites a vision to Earl of his guilt and shame: "I remember the floor—was yellow—I can see the floor and—her blood—her blood was smeared across it. I thought I'd killed her—but it was me. It was me I killed."[38] In the end, according to Matthew Roudané, "Henry Moss understands his source of spectral terror, discovers its etiology . . . the stimulus for terror ultimately comes from within."[39]

If *Henry Moss* represents Shepard's final meditation on the legacy of his own father, the conclusion might best be summed up by James Dickey's succinct phrase in his poem "Adultery": "Guilt is magic." It is guilt that connects Earl with his brother, and it is guilt that finally lets Henry rest in peace. It is also Earl's guilt that disconnects him from the trajectory his father followed, that allows him to choose a different path in life. Guilt motivates him to proclaim, "I am *nothing* like the old man! . . . We're as different as chalk and cheese."[40] *The Late Henry Moss* also emphasizes the importance of remembering, of how remembering opens up spaces for redemption and reconnection. The brothers' opening and closing lines, then, take on a whole new level of significance:

RAY: Well, you know me, Earl—I was never one to live in the past. That
   was never my deal. You know—You remember how I was.
EARL: Yeah. Yeah, right. I remember.[41]

Earl's final line (which, ironically, is also his first line of the play) suggests the importance of remembering: without memories, the final moments of his father's life would be lost. In *The Late Henry Moss*, the world of the past exists simultaneously with the world of the present. One informs the other.

Shepard has emphasized the connection between the past and the present by having memories of past actions take place in real time. Such a revision of temporal representation literally raises Henry from the dead and, in a sense, exorcises the ghosts of the family. *The Late Henry Moss* offers a final, satisfying conclusion to almost thirty years of work on the slipperiness of familial identity, competing masculinities, emotional inheritance, and the weight of the past on the present world.

Shepard's final two plays of the decade—*Kicking a Dead Horse* (2007) and *Ages of the Moon* (2009)—are much simpler in scope than *The Late Henry Moss*. *Kicking a Dead Horse* is a play sustained entirely by one actor, while *Ages of the Moon* concerns interactions between two men. In *Kicking a Dead Horse*, we meet Hobart Struther, an art dealer who became rich by buying cheap paintings in Wyoming saloons and selling them to high class art collectors for millions of dollars. Desperate for some kind of authentic experience, Hobart sets out on a journey into the desert with his horse, but when the animal passes away, he is stranded. Alone, he creates conversations among different personalities about his quest to discover how to live authentically. *Ages of the Moon* hearkens back to the world of Beckett, especially *Waiting for Godot* as two aging men spend the majority of the time onstage talking back and forth without concluding anything. Cantankerous Ames sends for his oldest friend, Byron, to come and keep him company; it seems Ames has just been "banished" by his wife after she discovers proof that he has had an affair. The men meet and drink on Ames's front porch and talk about an upcoming lunar eclipse. Together, they talk, fight, shout, and come to terms with each other after years of absence.

Both pieces are written, it seems, for one actor, Stephen Rea, who became a legitimate pop culture phenomenon after his performance in the movie *The Crying Game*. Shepard dedicated *Kicking a Dead Horse* to Rea, who wrote in the introduction to the piece about Shepard's contribution to the American stage: "The plays of Sam Shepard, more than any writer since Beckett, feel like musical experiences. They transcend meaning, avoid the literary and conceptual, and search for a concrete immediate reality, beyond the idea, which the actor and audience are forced to experience directly. . . . Beckett said of Joyce, 'His writing is not about something. It is something.' That, of course, is Sam Shepard's achievement."[42] Sam Shepard has, indeed, achieved a great deal in his nearly forty-five-year career: first as the compelling figure of the off-off-Broadway movement, then as the cowboy poet of the American stage, and, finally, as a prolific, thoughtful, and mature actor, writer, and director. Shepard has written not only for the stage and screen, but his oeuvre contains short stories, essays, and creative nonfiction. In addition to his writing career, Shepard has also established himself as an actor of great merit, appearing in nearly sixty films, including popular performances in movies such as *The Right Stuff* (1983), *Snow Falling on Cedars* (1999), *The Notebook* (2004), and *Brothers* (2009).

But his achievement in drama deserves primary attention, for Shepard has created some of the most memorable and compelling drama in the history of the American stage. His plays challenge audiences and scholars alike to reconsider the possibilities of theater as a shared and collaborative event, and his work investigates the most difficult of all puzzles: identity itself. Whether interrogating notions of masculinity within the competitive American family or demythologizing sites of cultural memory, Sam Shepard continues to contest and revise American identity with each passing decade.

NOTES

Chapter 1—Understanding Sam Shepard

   1. Shepard, "Language, Visualization and the Inner Library," 219.

   2. Chubb, "Metaphors, Mad Dogs and Old Time Cowboys," 187.

   3. Ibid., 188.

   4. Quoted in Shewey, *Sam Shepard*, 18.

   5. Chubb, "Metaphors, Mad Dogs and Old Time Cowboys," 188–89, 189.

   6. Ibid., 190.

   7. Quoted in Shewey, *Sam Shepard*, 24.

   8. Chubb, "Metaphors, Mad Dogs and Old Time Cowboys," 190.

   9. Ibid., 191.

  10. Ibid., 190.

  11. Michael Smith, "Theatre: *Cowboys* and *The Rock Garden.*" *Village Voice*, October 22, 1964, 13.

  12. Chubb, "Metaphors, Mad Dogs and Old Time Cowboys," 191.

  13. Ibid., 193.

  14. Shewey, *Sam Shepard*, 45.

  15. Chubb, "Metaphors, Mad Dogs and Old Time Cowboys," 198.

  16. Shewey, *Sam Shepard*, 48.

  17. Chubb, "Metaphors, Mad Dogs and Old Time Cowboys," 194.

  18. Shewey, *Sam Shepard*, 55.

  19. Ibid., 73.

  20. Chubb, "Metaphors, Mad Dogs and Old Time Cowboys," 201.

  21. Ibid., 200.

  22. Shewey, *Sam Shepard*, 83–84.

  23. Chubb, "Metaphors, Mad Dogs and Old Time Cowboys," 201.

  24. Ibid., 205.

  25. Quoted in Shewey, *Sam Shepard*, 102.

  26. Ibid., 107.

  27. Ibid., 108.

  28. Ibid., 109.

  29. Ibid., 114.

  30. Ibid., 115.

  31. Ibid., 122.

  32. Amy Lippman, "Rhythm and Truths: An Interview with Sam Shepard by Amy Lippman," in *The American Theatre Reader: Essays and Conversations from*

"American Theatre" Magazine, Vol. 2 (New York: Theatre Communications Group, 2009), 133.

33. Quoted in Shewey, Sam Shepard, 132.
34. Ibid., 133.
35. Coe, "The Saga of Sam Shepard," 122.
36. Shewey, Sam Shepard, 142.
37. Ibid., 180.
38. Ibid., 181.
39. Rosen, Sam Shepard, 226.
40. Ibid., 235–36.
41. Shewey, Sam Shepard, 226.
42. Ibid., 228.

Chapter 2—Experimentations with Sound, Language, and Myth

1. Chubb, "Metaphors, Mad Dogs, and Old Time Cowboys," 190.
2. Ibid., 191.
3. Ibid., 202.
4. Marranca, "Alphabetical Shepard," 13.
5. Bottoms, The Theatre of Sam Shepard, 29.
6. Chubb, "Metaphors, Mad Dogs, and Old Time Cowboys," 193–94.
7. Bottoms, The Theatre of Sam Shepard, 24.
8. Chubb, "Metaphors, Mad Dogs, and Old Time Cowboys," 194.
9. Ibid.
10. Ibid., 197.
11. Shepard, "The Unseen Hand" and Other Plays, 203.
12. Bottoms, The Theatre of Sam Shepard, 125.
13. Shepard, "The Unseen Hand" and Other Plays, 233.
14. Bottoms, The Theatre of Sam Shepard, 52.
15. Shepard, Seven Plays, 261.
16. Ibid., 274.
17. Ibid., 265.
18. Ibid., 271.
19. Ibid., 278.
20. Ibid., 298.
21. Shepard, "Fool for Love" and Other Plays, 115.
22. Ibid., 116.
23. Shewey, Sam Shepard, 58.
24. Shepard, "The Unseen Hand" and Other Plays, 56.
25. Shewey, Sam Shepard, 60.
26. Shepard, "The Unseen Hand" and Other Plays, 8.
27. Shepard, Seven Plays, 214–15.
28. Ibid., 216.
29. Ibid., 219.
30. Ibid., 230.
31. Ibid., 230–31, 239.
32. Ibid., 241.
33. Ibid., 247.
34. Ibid., 232.

35. Ibid., 239–40.

36. Shepard, *"Fool for Love" and Other Plays*, 285.

37. Ibid., 287.

38. Ibid., 203–4.

39. Ibid., 205.

40. Ibid., 211.

41. Ibid., 216.

42. Ibid., 217–18.

43. Shewey, *Sam Shepard*, 106.

Chapter 3—Divining the Cure

1. Bottoms, *The Theatre of Sam Shepard*, 153.

2. Shepard, *Seven Plays*, 196.

3. Thomas P. Adler, "*Curse of the Starving Class*," review of *Curse of the Starving Class*, by Shepard, *Educational Theatre Journal* 29 (October 1977): 409.

4. Harold Clurman, "Theatre," review of *Curse of the Starving Class*, by Shepard, *Nation*, March 25, 1978, 348.

5. Ibid., 349.

6. Rehm Rush, "*Curse of the Starving Class*," review of *Curse of the Starving Class*, by Shepard, *Theatre Journal* 38 (May, 1986): 217.

7. Ibid., 218.

8. Shewey, *Sam Shepard*, 184.

9. Ibid., 191–92.

10. Alvin Klein, "About Sam Shepard's Kitchen," *New York Times*, February 20, 2000, 14, 17.

11. Bottoms, *The Theatre of Sam Shepard*, 154.

12. Shewey, *Sam Shepard*, 108.

13. Cott, "The *Rolling Stone* Interview," 172.

14. Shewey, *Sam Shepard*, 97.

15. Ibid., 108.

16. Terry Curtis Fox, "Family Plot," *Village Voice*, March 12, 1978, 77.

17. Bottoms, *The Theatre of Sam Shepard*, 158.

18. Charles R. Lyons, "Shepard's Family Trilogy and the Conventions of Modern Realism," in *Rereading Shepard: Contemporary Critical Essays on the Plays of Sam Shepard*, ed. Leonard Wilcox (New York: St. Martin's Press, 1993), 126.

19. Bottoms, *The Theatre of Sam Shepard*, 158.

20. Ibid., 157.

21. Shepard, *Seven Plays*, 185. Quotations from the play come from this text and are referenced parenthetically through the remainder of the chapter.

22. Bert Cardullo, "Shepard's *Curse of the Starving Class*," *Explicator* 42 (Fall 1983): 64.

23. William E. Kleb, "*Curse of the Starving Class* and the Logic of Destruction," *Contemporary Theatre Review* 8, no. 4 (1998): 12.

Chapter 4—Hidden Trespasses

1. Shepard, *Seven Plays*, 63. Quotations from the play come from this text and are referenced parenthetically through the remainder of the chapter.

2. Shewey, *Sam Shepard*, 124.

3. Ibid., 238

4. Coen, "Things at Stake Here," 28.

5. Ben Brantley, "A Sam Shepard Revival Gets Him to Broadway," *New York Times,* May 1, 1996, C15, 5.

6. Shepard, *Buried Child,* 21.

7. Ibid., 22

8. James R. Stacy, "Making the Grave Less Deep: A Descriptive Assessment of Sam Shepard's Revisions to *Buried Child,*" *Journal of American Drama and Theatre* 9 (Fall 1997): 62.

9. Coen, "Things at Stake Here," 28.

10. Stacy, "Making the Grave Less Deep," 65.

11. Shepard, *Buried Child* (1997 ed.), 32.

12. Stacy, "Making the Grave Less Deep," 65.

13. Ibid., 72.

14. Shewey, *Sam Shepard,* 122.

15. Thomas P. Adler, "Ghosts of Ibsen in Shepard's *Buried Child,*" *Notes on Modern American Literature* 1 (March 1986): item 3.

16. Shewey, *Sam Shepard,* 122.

17. Bert Cardullo, "Literary Allusions in Sam Shepard's *Buried Child.*" *Notes on Contemporary Literature* 39, no. 5 (2009): 1.

18. Laurin Porter, "Modern and Postmodern Wastelands: *Long Day's Journey into Night* and Shepard's *Buried Child,*" *Eugene O'Neill Review* 17 (March 3, 1993): 108.

19. Ibid., 117.

20. Cardullo, "Literary Allusions in Sam Shepard's *Buried Child,*" 3.

21. Ibid., 5.

Chapter 5 — The Authentic Family

1. Shepard, *Seven Plays,* 3. Quotations from the play come from this text and are referenced parenthetically through the remainder of the chapter.

2. Shewey, *Sam Shepard,* 131.

3. Rosen, *Sam Shepard,* 137.

4. Shewey, *Sam Shepard,* 131.

4. Ibid., 132.

5. Westgate, "Negotiating the American West," 732.

6. Ibid., 734.

7. Rosen, *Sam Shepard,* 138.

8. Coe, "The Saga of Sam Shepard," 122.

9. Don Shewey, "The True Story of *True West,*" *Village Voice,* November 30, 198; quoted in Shewey's *Sam Shepard,* 136.

10. Shewey, *Sam Shepard,* 133.

Chapter 6 — Chaos and Connection

1. Amy Lippman, "Rhythm and Truths: An Interview with Sam Shepard by Amy Lippman," in *The American Theatre Reader: Essays and Conversations from "American Theatre" Magazine, Vol. 2* (New York: Theatre Communications Group, 2009), 136.

2. Shepard, *"Fool for Love" and Other Plays,* 19.

3. Ibid., 20.

4. Ibid., 40.

5. Quoted in Shewey, *Sam Shepard*, 141.

6. Shepard, *"Fool for Love" and Other Plays*, 35.

7. Ibid., 48.

8. Ibid., 54.

9. Ibid., 55.

10. Ibid., 27.

11. Ibid., 57.

12. Quoted in Shewey, *Sam Shepard*, 182.

13. Shepard, *A Lie of the Mind*, 37–38.

14. Ibid., 39.

15. Ibid., 36.

16. Ibid., 40.

17. Ibid., 131.

18. Ibid., 1.

19. Ibid., 41.

20. Ibid., 131.

21. Cott, "The *Rolling Stone* Interview," 170.

22. Shepard, *A Lie of the Mind*, 103–5.

23. Cott, "The *Rolling Stone* Interview," 200.

24. Jeremy Gerard, "*Simpatico*," review of *Simpatico*, by Shepard, *Daily Variety*, November 21, 1994, 44.

25. Leslie Wade, "*States of Shock, Simpatico,* and *Eyes for Consuela*: Sam Shepard's Plays of the 1990s," in *The Cambridge Companion to Sam Shepard*, ed. Matthew Roudané (New York: Cambridge University Press, 2002), 258.

26. Rosen,"Silent Tongues," 39.

27. Shepard, *"States of Shock"; "Far North"; "Silent Tongue,"* 12.

28. Ibid., 34.

29. Ibid., 42–43.

30. Ibid., 44.

31. Ibid., 26.

32. Ibid., 27.

33. Wade, "Sam Shepard's Plays of the 1990s," 266.

34. Michael Feingold, "Loner Stars," *Village Voice*, November 22, 1994, 77.

35. Wade, "Sam Shepard's Plays of the 1990s," 273.

36. Matthew Roudané, "Shepard on Shepard: An Interview," in *The Cambridge Companion to Sam Shepard*, ed. Matthew Roudané (New York: Cambridge University Press, 2002), 79–80.

37. Matthew Roudané, "Sam Shepard's *The Late Henry Moss*," in *The Cambridge Companion to Sam Shepard*, ed. Matthew Roudané (Cambridge University Press, 2002), 281.

38. Shepard, *The Late Henry Moss*, 112.

39. Roudané, "Sam Shepard's *The Late Henry Moss*," 288–89.

40. Shepard, *The Late Henry Moss*, 83.

41. Ibid., 113.

42. Shepard, *Kicking a Dead Horse*, 6.

SELECT BIBLIOGRAPHY

Works by Sam Shepard
Listed in order of publication

BOOKS

Five Plays. Indianapolis: Bobbs-Merrill, 1967.

La Turista: A Play in Two Acts. Indianapolis: Bobbs-Merrill, 1968.

Collision Course. Edited by Edward Parone. New York: Vintage, 1969 [contains the play *Cowboys #2*].

Oh! Calcutta! An Entertainment with Music. Edited by Kenneth Tynan. New York: Grove Press, 1969.

Maxagasm: A Distorted Western for Soul and Psyche. Los Angeles: Creative Management Associates, 1970.

Operation Sidewinder: A Play in Two Acts. Indianapolis: Bobbs-Merrill, 1970.

"The Unseen Hand" and Other Plays. Indianapolis: Bobbs-Merrill, 1971.

"Mad Dog Blues" and Other Plays. New York: Winter House, 1972.

Zabriskie Point. New York: Simon and Schuster, 1972 [with Michelangelo Antonioni, Fred Gardner, Tonino Guerra, and Clare Peploe].

Hawk Moon: A Book of Short Stories, Poems and Monologues. Los Angeles: Black Sparrow, 1973.

"The Tooth of Crime" and "Geography of a Horse Dreamer." New York: Grove Press, 1974.

"Action" and "The Unseen Hand": Two Plays. London: Faber and Faber, 1975.

"Angel City," "Curse of the Starving Class," and Other Plays. New York: Urizen Books, 1976.

Rolling Thunder Logbook. New York: Viking Press, 1977.

Suicide in B-flat: A Mysterious Overture. New York: Berman, 1978.

"Buried Child" and "Seduced" and "Suicide in B-flat." New York: Urizen Books, 1979.

Four Two-Act Plays. New York: Urizen Books, 1980.

Sam Shepard: Seven Plays. New York: Bantam Books, 1981.

True West. New York: French, 1981.

Motel Chronicles. San Francisco: City Lights, 1982.

"Fool for Love" and "The Sad Lament of Pecos Bill on the Eve of Killing His Wife." San Francisco: City Lights, 1983.

"Fool for Love" and Other Plays. New York: Bantam, 1984.

Paris, Texas. New York: Ecco Press, 1984.

"The Unseen Hand" and Other Plays. New York: Bantam, 1986.
A Lie of the Mind. New York: Plume, 1987.
"A Lie of the Mind: A Play in Three Acts" and "The War in Heaven: Angel's Mono-
  logue." New York: New American Library, 1987. [The War in Heaven with Joseph
  Chaikin]
Joseph Chaikin & Sam Shepard: Letters and Texts, 1972—1984. Edited by Barry V.
  Daniels. New York: New American Library, 1989.
"States of Shock"; "Far North"; "Silent Tongue": A Play and Two Screenplays. New
  York: Vintage, 1993.
Simpatico: A Play in Three Acts. London: Methuen, 1995.
Cruising Paradise: Tales. New York: Knopf, 1996.
Buried Child. New York: Dramatists Play Service, 1997.
Great Dream of Heaven: Stories. New York: Knopf, 2002.
"The Late Henry Moss"; "Eyes for Consuela"; "When the World Was Green": Three
  Plays. New York: Vintage, 2002.
The God of Hell: A Play. New York: Vintage Books, 2005.
Kicking a Dead Horse: A Play. New York: Vintage, 2008.
Day Out of Days: Stories. New York: Alfred A. Knopf, 2010.

SELECTED ESSAYS

"Sam Shepard." In The New Underground Theatre. edited by Robert J. Schroeder,
  79–80. New York: Bantam, 1968.
Untitled. News of the American Place Theatre 3 (April 1971): 1–2.
"News Blues" Time Out, July 12–18, 1974, 16–17.
"Emotional Tyranny." Theatre Quarterly 4 (August–October 1974): 22.
"Language, Visualization and the Inner Library." Drama Review 21 (December
  1977): 49–58. Reprinted in American Dreams: The Imagination of Sam Shepard,
  edited by Bonnie Marranca, 214–19. New York: Performing Arts Journal, 1981.
"True Dylan." Esquire, July 1987, 57–68.

SELECTED INTERVIEWS

Allen, Jennifer. "The Man on the High Horse." Esquire, November 1988, 141–44.
Brantley, Ben. "Sam Shepard, Storyteller." New York Times, November 13, 1994,
  H1, H26.
Cadwalladr, Carole. "Sam Shepard Opens Up." Observer (London), March 20, 2010,
  11.
Chubb, Kenneth. "Metaphors, Mad Dogs and Old Time Cowboys." In American
  Dreams: The Imagination of Sam Shepard, edited by Bonnie Marranca, 187–209.
  New York: Performing Arts Journal Publications, 1981.
Coe, Robert. "The Saga of Sam Shepard." New York Times Magazine, November 23,
  1980, 56–58, 118–24.
Coen, Stephanie. "Things at Stake Here." In Contemporary Literary Criticism, edited
  by Janet Witalec, 28. Detroit: Gale, 2003.
Cott, Jonathan. "The Rolling Stone Interview: Sam Shepard." Rolling Stone,
  December 18, 1986–January 1, 1987, 166, 168, 170, 172, 198, 200.
Dark, John. "The 'True West' Interviews." West Coast Plays 9 (Summer 1981):
  51–71.
Fay, Stephen. "The Silent Type." Vogue, February 1985, 213–18.

Freedman, Samuel G. "Sam Shepard and the Mythic Family." *New York Times*, December 1, 1985, sect. 2, pp. 1, 20.

Gussow, Mel. "Sam Shepard: Writer on the Way Up." *New York Times*, November 12, 1969, 42.

Kakutani, Michiko. "Myths, Dreams, Realities—Sam Shepard's America." *New York Times*, January 29, 1984, B1, B26–28.

Lippman, Amy. "A Conversation with Sam Shepard." *Harvard Advocate*, March 1983, 2–6, 44–46.

Rosen, Carol. "Silent Tongues: Sam Shepard's Exploration of Emotional Territory." *Village Voice*, August 4, 1992, 34–42.

Roudané, Matthew. "Shepard on Shepard; An Interview." In *The Cambridge Companion to Sam Shepard*, edited by Matthew Roudané, 64–80. New York: Cambridge University Press, 2002.

Sessums, Kevin. "Sam Shepard: Geography of a Horse Dreamer." *Interview*, September 1988, 7–78.

Shewey, Don. "Patriot Acts." *Village Voice*, November 9, 2004, http://www.villagevoice.com/2004-11-09/news/patriot-acts/.

Shewey, Don. "Rock-and-Roll Jesus with a Cowboy Mouth." *American Theatre* 21 (April 2004): 20–84.

VerMeulen, Michael. "Sam Shepard, Yes, Yes, Yes." *Esquire*, February, 1980, 79–81, 85–86.

White, Michael. "Underground Landscapes." *Manchester Guardian*, February 20, 1974, 8.

Secondary Sources

BIOGRAPHIES

Oumano, Ellen. *Sam Shepard: The Life and Work of an American Dreamer*. New York: St. Martin's Press, 1986.

Shewey, Don. *Sam Shepard*. New York: Da Capo Press, 1997.

Tucker, Martin. *Sam Shepard*. New York: Continuum, 1992.

BOOK-LENGTH LITERARY CRITICISM

Benet, Carol. *Sam Shepard on the German Stage: Critics, Politics, Myths*. New York: Peter Lang, 1993.

Bloom, Harold, ed. *Sam Shepard*. Bloom's Major Dramatists. Philadelphia: Chelsea House, 2003.

Bottoms, Stephen J. *The Theatre of Sam Shepard: States of Crisis*. New York: Cambridge University Press, 1998.

Callens, Johan. *Dis/figuring Sam Shepard*. New York: Lang, 2007.

DeRose, David J. *Sam Shepard*. New York: Twayne, 1992.

Graham, Laura J. *Sam Shepard: Theme, Image, and the Director*. New York: Lang, 1995.

Hart, Lynda. *Sam Shepard's Metaphorical Stages*. Westport, Conn.: Greenwood Press, 1987.

King, Kimball, ed. *Sam Shepard: A Casebook*. New York: Garland, 1988.

Marranca, Bonnie, ed. *American Dreams: The Imagination of Sam Shepard*. New York: Performing Arts Journal Publications, 1981.

McGhee, Jim. *True Lies: The Architecture of the Fantastic in the Plays of Sam Shepard*. New York: Lang, 1993.

Mottram, Ron. *Inner Landscapes: The Theater of Sam Shepard*. Columbia: University of Missouri Press, 1984.

Roudané, Matthew, ed. *The Cambridge Companion to Sam Shepard*. New York: Cambridge University Press, 2002.

Rosen, Carol. *Sam Shepard: A "Poetic Rodeo."* New York: Palgrave, 2004.

Taav, Michael. *A Body across the Map: The Father-Son Plays of Sam Shepard*. New York: Lang, 1999.

Tucker, Martin. *Sam Shepard*. New York: Continuum, 1992.

Wade, Leslie A. *Sam Shepard and the American Theatre*. Westport, Conn.: Greenwood Press, 1997.

Wilcox, Leonard, ed. *Rereading Shepard: Contemporary Critical Essays on the Plays of Sam Shepard*. New York: St. Martin's Press, 1993.

CRITICAL ESSAYS

Bachman, Charles R. "Defusion of Menace in the Plays of Sam Shepard." *Modern Drama* 19, (December 1976): 405–16.

Brater, Enoch. "American Clocks: Sam Shepard's Time Plays." *Modern Drama* 37 (Winter 1994): 603–12.

Cima, Jay Gibson. "Shifting Perspectives: Combining Shepard and Rauschenberg." *Theatre Journal* 38, no. 1 (1986): 67–81.

DeRose, David J. "Indian Country: Sam Shepard and the Cultural Other." *Contemporary Theatre Review* 8, no. 4 (1998): 55–73.

Garner, Stanton B., Jr. "Staging 'Things': Realism and the Theatrical Object in Shepard's Theatre." *Contemporary Theatre Review* 8, no. 3 (1998): 55–66.

Haney, William S., II. "Artistic Expression, Intimacy, and the Primal Holon: Sam Shepard's *Suicide in B-flat* and *The Tooth of Crime*." *disClosure*, no. 15 (2006): 71–92.

Heilman, Robert B. "Shepard's Plays: Stylistic and Thematic Ties." *Sewanee Review* 100 (Fall 1992): 630–44.

Hoeper, Jeffrey D. "Cain, Canaanites, and Philistines in Sam Shepard's *True West*." *Modern Drama* 36 (March 1993): 76–82.

Lanier, Gregory W. "Two Opposite Animals: Structural Pairing in Sam Shepard's *A Lie of the Mind*." *Modern Drama* 34 (September 1991): 410–21.

Larsen, Darl. "There Is No Place Like Home: American Affirmation in Sam Shepard's *Unseen Hand*." *Journal of Popular Culture* 42 (October 2009): 875–89.

Lion, John. "Rock 'n Roll Jesus with a Cowboy Mouth: Sam Shepard Is the Inkblot of the '80s." *American Theatre* 1 (April 1984): 4–8.

Marranca, Bonnie. "Alphabetical Shepard: The Play of Words." In *American Dreams: The Imagination of Sam Shepard*, edited by Bonnie Marranca, 13–33. New York: Performing Arts Publications, 1981.

Opipari, Benjamin. "Shhhhhhame: Silencing the Family Secret in Sam Shepard's *Buried Child*." *Style* 44 (Spring/Summer 2010): 123–38.

Putzel, Steven. "An American Cowboy on the English Fringe: Sam Shepard's London Audience." *Modern Drama* 36 (March 1993): 131–46.

Schechner, Richard. "Drama, Script, Theatre, Performance." *Drama Review* 17 (September 1973): 5–36.

Schvey, Henry I. "A Worm in the Wood: The Father-Son Relationship in the Plays of Sam Shepard." *Modern Drama* 36 (March 1993): 12–26.

Sparr, Landy F. "Sam Shepard and the Dysfunctional American Family: Therapeutic Perspectives." *American Journal of Psychotherapy* 44 (October 1990): 563–76.

Westgate, J. Chris. "Negotiating the American West in Sam Shepard's Family Plays." *Modern Drama* 48 (Winter 2005): 726–43.

Wetzsteon, Ross. "Sam Shepard: Escape Artist." *Partisan Review* 49, no. 2 (1982): 253–61.

Whiting, Charles G. "Images of Women in Shepard's Theatre." *Modern Drama* 33 (December 1990): 494–506.

Willadt, Susanne. "States of War in Sam Shepard's *States of Shock.*" *Modern Drama* 36 (March 1993): 147–66.

Williams, Megan. "Nowhere Man and the Twentieth-Century Cowboy: Images of Identity and American History in Sam Shepard's *True West.*" *Modern Drama* 40 (Spring 1997): 57–73.

Wynands, Sandra. "Sam Shepard's Anti-Western *Silent Tongue* as Cultural Critique." *Canadian Review of American Studies* 35, no. 3 (2005): 299–313.

INDEX